SECRETARIES OF THE MOON

SECRETARIES OF THE MOON

THE LETTERS OF WALLACE STEVENS

& JOSÉ RODRÍGUEZ FEO

Edited by Beverly Coyle and

Alan Filreis

Duke University Press

Durham 1986

PS
3537
T4753
Z496
1986

2/1987
Am. Lit.

Permission to reprint has been granted by the following:
R. P. Blackmur Papers (Box 1, Folder 11; Box 8,
Folder 9) published with permission of Princeton
University Library.
Letters from the Wallace Stevens Manuscripts published
by permission of the Houghton Library.
Letters from José Rodríguez Feo to Wallace Stevens,
WAS 1588-1638, reproduced by permission of
The Huntington Library, San Marino, California.
From Letters of Wallace Stevens, by Wallace Stevens,
edited by Holly Stevens. Copyright ©1966 by Holly
Stevens. Reprinted by permission of Alfred A. Knopf,
Inc. and Faber and Faber Limited.

CONTENTS

ACKNOWLEDGMENTS

In putting together the decade of correspondence between a major American poet and a young Cuban critic, we hope to reintroduce Wallace Stevens to our readers as an engaged, even excited, respondent. If we succeed, it will be in large part due to Holly Stevens, whose careful editing of her father's letters twenty years ago first indicated the poet's brilliance as a correspondent. We are extremely grateful to Miss Stevens.

There are many others who encouraged us in this project and helped us see it to publication. We wish to recognize the special efforts of A. Walton Litz, Peter Brazeau, Milton Bates, the late Samuel French Morse, and, of course, José Rodríguez Feo himself.

For their patience and skill with early versions of our introduction and commentary, we are indebted to J. C. Levenson and Raymond Nelson of the University of Virginia, and Ann Imbrie of Vassar College. We would also like to thank Maria Theresa Meyer, Marci Sternheim, Andrew Bush, and Sienah Wold for their help with the difficult Spanish of the *Orígenes* writers; Edward Fuhr, Catherine Robbins, and Henry Ross, who helped at various stages of the editing; Sandra Levinson, at the Center for Cuban Studies, who helped facilitate our interviews with Mr. Rodríguez Feo in 1983; and Sara Hodson and Melanie Wizner for help with the archives at the Huntington and the Houghton Libraries respectively.

A NOTE ON THE TEXT

This volume contains all ninety-eight extant letters between Wallace Stevens and José Rodríguez Feo. Fifty-four are from the younger man to the poet, and they are published here for the first time by permission of The Huntington Library and Mr. Rodríguez Feo, who is referred to throughout as "José."

In 1966 Holly Stevens edited, with some excisions, thirty-seven of her father's letters to José in *Letters of Wallace Stevens* (Alfred A. Knopf). Those letters are republished here, with all omitted passages restored, by permission of Knopf; they are housed at the Houghton Library, Harvard University. Carbon copies of these letters and all the original letters from José are part of the Wallace Stevens holdings at The Huntington Library, San Marino, California. Ten previously unpublished letters from Stevens are included by permission of Miss Stevens and Harvard University. We are also grateful to Princeton University Library for granting us permission to quote briefly from unpublished letters in the Allen Tate and R. P. Blackmur Papers.

Inadvertent misspellings and typographical errors have been silently corrected in José's side of the correspondence. But errors that may have had even the smallest substantive interest to Stevens have been preserved. For example, the word "assist" was not changed to "attend" even though José himself might have made the correction on a second glance. His command of English is superb. His use of the word "usufruct" may well send native speakers to the dictionary for edification. Nevertheless, he made many interesting mistakes, some of which may have been intended— "Merry Eastern" for "Happy Easter" in a letter written one April, the phrase "the slappiest of arrangements" to describe the disorganization of American culture, or the query "Does it mathers that I know him [Professor Frank Mather]?" Such choices, intended or accidental, are inseparable from the liveliness of his English.

A question mark in brackets [?] indicates either the omission of a word or phrase or some missing piece of information. Book and magazine titles are italicized and titles of poems are placed in quotations to avoid confusion, but other unnecessary forms of standardization are avoided. Foreign words, for example, are only italicized when José underscored them himself.

The following key is used for quotations from editions of Stevens' work published by Alfred A. Knopf, Inc.:

CP   *The Collected Poems of Wallace Stevens* (1954)
L   *Letters of Wallace Stevens,* edited by Holly Stevens (1966)
NA   *The Necessary Angel: Essays on Reality and the Imagination* (1951)
OP   *Opus Posthumous,* edited, with an introduction, by Samuel French Morse (1957)

Page numbers to these editions appear in parentheses in the text; bracketed dates refer to letters in this volume; a parenthetical (HS) in the footnotes indicates a direct quotation or adaptation of Miss Stevens' notation from the *Letters.*

INTRODUCTION

The moon which moves around over Havana these nights like a waitress serving drinks, moves around over Connecticut the same nights like someone poisoning her husband.
Stevens to Rodríguez Feo [28 October 1949]

In the last ten years of his life, Wallace Stevens corresponded with José Rodríguez Feo, an irresistible young Cuban, who launched their friendship in late 1944 with this remarkable sentence: "With such ardour one must be allowed the picadillo of forgetting that after all there is a due respect to the author."

He wrote to ask permission to publish some poems in translation for his literary review, *Orígenes,* and Stevens was apparently delighted with more than the request. He immediately began writing to "Mr. Rodríguez Feo"—later "Dear José," "Dear Caribbean," "Dear Antillean"—and in less than a year confided to others that the Cuban was now his "most exciting correspondent." Stevens described him as "an isolated young man . . . reaching out for responsive contacts," a well-read pastoral figure with "his garden, his mule and cow and his negro cook":

> I speak of him because if you [James Guthrie], living in England, are conscious of the tensions that exist in the world today, you might like to feel that there are still young men of letters, even to be found in the Caribbean, studying and creating and doing it in peace without any sense of anxiety as to the present or as to the future. (*L,* 515)

The twenty-four-year-old José was at least in a state of flux, if not anxiety, as he read and studied on his mother's sugar plantation, and Stevens' description of his placid life must suggest a considerable degree of projection on the poet's part. In fact, José had unfinished business in North America where he had been educated since the age of ten, where he had an older brother already married to a New Yorker, where encouraging professors were interested in his academic prospects.

After almost two years of correspondence, Stevens would come to recognize José more accurately and find himself somewhat troubled to learn that sometime in September 1946 he ran the risk of meeting the young man in person. Their common interests had been fully rehearsed in the steady exchange of questions and anecdotes—their Harvard education, their enduring admiration for George Santayana and his understanding of things tropical versus things New England, their cooperative spirit in seeing Stevens' poems translated for a Cuban audience. But the practical reality of these shared values would not have been obvious to Stevens at his office in Hartford. Nor would their meeting have appealed, for the moment, to his imagination that so delighted in knowing people at a distance but feared the necessary adjustments actual confrontation required.

Herein lies one of the sad, if somewhat amusing, stories that emerges from these wonderful letters. Stevens' aversion to bridging natural distances between himself and acquaintances by mail is well known. We know, for example, of his reluctance to give anything other than a business address to his long-standing correspondent, Henry Church, who remained "Dear Mr. Church" for the entire eight years of their exchange. On rare occasions Stevens expressed his fears in this regard with a comic self-deprecation related to the formalities of the Hartford Casualty and Indemnity Company of which he was a vice president. Writing to editor Ronald Latimer about an announced visit from a mutual acquaintance, Stevens trusted the discretion of Latimer and perhaps sent a friendly warning at the same time:

> Confidentially, he suggested that he and his wife would be touring this part of the world on foot and *in shorts* before

long, and promised to call on me. The office here is a solemn
affair of granite, with a portico resting on five of the grimmest
possible columns. The idea of Mr. Ney and his wife toddling
up the steps and asking for me made me suggest that they
might like to stop at some nearby resthouse and change to
something more bourgeois. This is merely one of the hilarious
possibilities of being in the insurance business. (*L,* 283)

José was far less likely to arrive in shorts than he was to arrive
wearing one of "the lovely ties" Stevens had sent him in Cuba,
which no doubt were appropriate ties for presentation at the Hartford. The anticipation Stevens must have felt in the case of José's
visit involved the possibly inappropriate claims of friendship and
familiarity. When José wrote from Cuba to invite himself, he as-
sumed incorrectly that he might get to know Stevens' life in Hartford in the same way Stevens wanted so urgently to know the par-
ticulars of his at villa Olga—his interaction with the silent cook, his
mother's charming comments about Stalin, the temperament of his
mule, Pompilio. Unfortunately he left home just missing Stevens'
instructional letter insisting that they meet in Manhattan instead of
on Stevens' own turf, and by the end of this particular visit to the
States accident and design conspired against José, playing out for
him "the hilarious possibilities" of trying to be friends with Wallace
Stevens. What followed was a month-long comedy of errors involving an exchange of four letters, at least one phone call, and three
near misses.

As planned, José proceeded first to Vermont to assist in a summer language program at Middlebury College. From there he wrote
to Stevens on 25 August that he would stop briefly in Boston before
heading in Stevens' direction. By the time Stevens received this message there would be no way to head off the young man. Two days
later, on the twenty-seventh, José wrote again that he planned to
visit Stevens at his office in the next week. Despite its pretense of
being businesslike and precise, the note captures the spirit of his
other letters—playful, inexact (he forgets to name the day), and
comically meditative:

It shall be *exactly* at noon so as to trap the poet as he exits
from the walled citadel of the insurances. . . . Imagine what

would occur if I were to be delayed in my schedule. I would
find you gone; lost for three quarters of an hour. I am motoring; . . . I shall detail *precisely* the route so as not to confirm
the old Gothic invention of manana and retarded overtures.
What a triumph; to immortalize with twelve bells the fame of
my timelessness. [27 August 1946]

This letter would have reached the Hartford by Friday, 30 August. Stevens may or may not have comprehended its message. He
had planned a brief and uncharacteristic vacation with his wife. He
intended to be away from that Friday until the next Monday (only
five workdays away from the desk) and he would have plenty of
time to return home and travel back by train to Manhattan to meet
up with José, which, he had said in the letter he sent to Cuba, he
very much wanted to do. Later correspondence reveals that he knew
José would be staying at the Stanhope and would not leave the
country until 23 September.

José tried everything possible when he arrived "at noon" and
found the poet gone. His effort included an abortive phone call to
Stevens' resort in Hershey. Through a bad connection the two men
apparently had difficulty straightening anything out. On this particular visit to Hershey and then Reading, Stevens became involved
in new genealogical research into his mother's family.[1] He extended
his rare vacation with Elsie from ten to twenty-five days, arriving in
Manhattan on 24 September, the day after José had left: "I called
up the Stanhope, which *confirmed* your departure [emphasis
added]." Some complex aversion on the part of Stevens may or may
not figure here as it obviously does in other instances involving acquaintances who attempted to meet him. He did seem to regret
missing José, but wrote to say so a week later in overly apologetic
tones in which he is unnecessarily repetitious and for the first time
protectively plural [2 October 1946].

1. See Stevens' letter of 30 September 1946 to Charles R. Barker (*L*,
534), in which he partially describes his research into Zeller family history during the last month. According to Peter Brazeau, Stevens also
had a reunion with his old friend, Judge Arthur Powell, on this same trip
to Pennsylvania. *Parts of a World: Wallace Stevens Remembered* (New
York: Random House, 1983), 112.

José received Stevens' explanation along with a poem, "Attempt to Discover Life," which had developed in Stevens' mind directly from José's reference to his sulfur-bath resort, San Miguel de los Baños. Whether Stevens meant it as such, the Cuban accepted the poem as the much warmer part of his apology. As consolation for having missed the poet in his element, here was new and eloquent proof that Stevens could intimately imagine José in *his*. José was grateful. "How very fine of you, to pay homage to our little local villages. . . . How magical the discovery!"

> The green roses drifted up from the table
> In smoke. The blue petals became
> The yellowing fomentations of effulgence . . .
> (*CP*, 370)

The descriptions in the poem had been achieved at so great a distance that it seemed to carry some message on the nature of their friendship. José wrote, "How can you see from so far-off those touching scenes?" Now, moved by what he interpreted as intimacy on Stevens' part, José translated the poem for *Orígenes* himself (rather than have someone else in his group do it, as had been the case with earlier submissions), and in his letter of 30 November wrote to thank Stevens.

This letter is the most moving and personal of the seventeen letters he had written by then. Here he alludes to a number of private matters very much on his mind, but without a doubt generously absolves Stevens of any miscues while consoling himself with the exchange of ideas, poetry, and meditations which perhaps only letters allow:

> My life flows as usual. I write, read and frequent the company of a few and selected amigos. I am as lonely as ever and yet quite happy in my isolation. All the vines are in bloom now, and looking across its flowery branches I see the sky remains blue and shining up there. What more can you ask of life? To open one's eyes in the morning and see only flowers and the open spaces blue and white above. And to read kind, friendly messages from our friends below. It doesn't signify that we

avert suffering and misery, all that is within us, but we must remain platonic and make the best of the little things the gods so kindly offer us every day: be it in the vision of a violet bouganville or the song of a banana vendor. I think that this is wisdom, not cowardice. I prefer to be foolish in those little things; not be made a fool reaching for the stars. [30 November 1946]

Stevens' brief reply to these sentiments must have come as still another disappointment. Answering only the direct question about "Attempt to Discover Life"—José had asked, in passing, "[W]hat are Hermosas?"—Stevens avoids the difficult questions concerning the meaning of his poem in relation to their friendship. He flatly answers: "Hermosas are a variety of roses." A man of few willing words when confronted, Stevens could be just that expository. Even in his generous letter of 19 December, he takes up none of the issues José raised about his loneliness, his consoling "platonism," the disappointment in his visit to the United States. The image of José's resort, San Miguel de los Baños, Stevens now wrote, had not been intended to suggest his physical response to people, to a Cuban as opposed, say, to a Mexican or Argentine. On the contrary, his poem referred to an entirely unreal place. In this sense of course Stevens did respond, making quick work indeed of the younger man's emphasis on the physical quality of an idea, or fact of life, with which Stevens had great trouble. Whatever disappointment he felt about Stevens' intentions, José did proceed to publish his rendering of "Attempt to Discover Life." It appeared that winter in the twelfth issue of *Orígenes* as "Tentativa por Descubrir La Vida."

It was not the first of Stevens' poems José translated. He had begun with "Notes Toward a Supreme Fiction" and several poems from *Harmonium* while a student at Harvard. At the same time he tried his hand at translating William Carlos Williams and Marianne Moore, becoming briefly a correspondent of each; he also corresponded with Elizabeth Bishop and Allen Tate. When he wrote to Stevens for the first time in November 1944, proposing to publish a version of "Esthétique" for his new review, he was confident that Williams would promote him as a translator should Stevens have any doubts. In *Orígenes* that year, José's rendition of "The Bitter World of Spring" was the first translation of Williams into Spanish.[2]

American English was more than a second language to José. Born in Havana in 1920 to a landed family, at age ten he came to the United States and was enrolled at the Fork Union Military Academy in Virginia, then at a parochial school in Summit, New Jersey, and was graduated from Choate in Wallingford, Connecticut. José's father had died when the boy was very young. His mother endured a lifetime of mental illness, and in later years her unstable health and periodic stays in sanitoria always provided José with a strong reason for returning to Cuba after successive attempts at making a life of his own in the United States. For months at a time, however, his mother could be a splendid companion. Seeing her now as a clairvoyant, now as a woman of profound misapprehension, José carefully related her comings and goings to Stevens, providing the disinterested man from Hartford true moments of pleasure, hilarity, and—what was rarer still—engagement.

From 1939 to 1943 José attended Harvard, Stevens' alma mater. There he heard Pedro Henríquez Ureña deliver the Charles Eliot Norton lectures (published in 1943 as the classic *Literary Currents in Hispanic America*) and sought the older man's friendship. Henríquez Ureña, who had written on and was fascinated by William James and George Santayana, helped focus José's interests in American letters. It was no doubt he who alerted José to Santayana's special case, a man caught physically and philosophically between the tenderness of the South and the sexlessness of the North. Later, just before Henríquez Ureña's death in 1946, José would be invited to work with him at the Institute of Philology in Buenos Aires. In the spring of 1943 José took his B.S. from Harvard and returned to Havana, where he intended to found and fund *Orígenes: Revista de arte y literatura.*

Orígenes and José's correspondence with Wallace Stevens span exactly the same decade, 1944 to 1954. Not long after José wrote Stevens for the first time, *Orígenes* contained first appearances of four of Stevens' new poems, accompanied by Spanish translations

2. "El Mundo Amargo de la Primavera," *Orígenes* 1, no. 3 (Fall 1944): 22–23. It was also the first appearance of the poem anywhere; *Orígenes* carried the English on a facing page.

by José's friend, Oscar Rodríguez Felíu: "Thinking of a Relation between the Images of Metaphors" ("Unidad de las Imagenes"), "Chaos in Motion and Not in Motion" ("El Caos Movil e Inmovil"), "The House Was Quiet and the World Was Calm" ("La Casa y el Mundo en Calma"), and "Continual Conservation with a Silent Man" ("Conversación con un Hombre Silencioso").

José and his associate editors put out thirty-six handsome outsized numbers of *Orígenes: Revista de arte y literatura* in this decade. More than perhaps any literary journal in the twentieth century, *Orígenes* was the organ of a group. The "Orígenes Group," as they are known, consisted of José, the poets Eliseo Diego, Cintio Vitier, José Lezama Lima, Angel Gaztelu, Fiña García Marruz, and Lorenzo García Vega, and the painter Mariano Rodríguez. José Rodríguez Feo was a competent and energetic editor; his contacts were extensive. He solicited contributions from F. O. Matthiessen and Harry Levin (both of whom he had known at Harvard), T. S. Eliot and Stephen Spender (he met both), Katherine Anne Porter, Elizabeth Bishop, Allen Tate, Alfonso Reyes, W. H. Auden, Albert Camus, Thomas Merton, Anaïs Nin, and Stevens' friends Walter Pach and James Johnson Sweeney. José himself contributed essays on Santayana, André Gide, Pedro Salinas, and Melville; a short story; translations of poetry by Stevens, Williams, Louis Aragon, Spender, and Eliot ("East Coker" and "Burnt Norton," both with Eliot's urging). He also translated James on Balzac, Camus on Nietzsche, Levin on Joyce, Auden on Lawrence, Theodore Spencer on Stephen Hero, Matthiessen on Eliot, and Santayana on himself.

In a statement of purpose introducing the first number of *Orígenes,* the editors explained the name of the journal by referring to their interest in soliciting and publishing poems and essays that reveal the artist in the act of formulating his ideas, "those moments of creation in which the seed becomes a being and the unknown becomes possessed insofar as is possible and does not engender an unfortunate arrogance."[3] In this sense the Orígenes Group *did* dismiss pure art, though they would still be accused of

3. ". . . aquellos momentos de creación en los que el germen se convierte en criatura y lo desconocido va siendo poseído en la medida en que esto es posible y en que no engendra una desdichada arrogancia." *Orígenes* 1, no. 1 (Spring 1944): 5.

loving it. They wanted to publish impure poems. They wanted to print art in formation, to find the moment when unconsciousness became conscious. Eight years later, the greatest poet in their group, Lezama Lima, was proud that they had printed the portion of Santayana's previously unpublished autobiography. And following Lezama Lima's idea that they must strive to universalize,[4] José, both as editor of *Orígenes* and especially as a devoted correspondent of Stevens, broke through two barriers the latter had set up to block his contact with others: location and generation.

Of course, Stevens had long ago discovered for himself the importance of correspondents to help him let down the first barrier; as his most important epistolary friend, José repeatedly drew forth and helped shape into a thematic element Stevens' belief in the transcendence of place. The crossing of generations, however—what Santayana had done in befriending Stevens at Harvard and José did by soliciting this correspondence—was out of Stevens' ken. On the other hand, José himself was idealized by the members of his group for spanning the gap between generations and nationalities. Lezama Lima wrote a retrospective of *Orígenes* in 1952 featuring this phenomenon. There he praised the members of the Orígenes Group for their ability to find affinities between their own youthful expressions and those of someone as cosmopolitan as George Santayana; he singles out José for inspiring a poem by Wallace Stevens in which the details, "the unthought-of groupings," "the far-off poetic imagination," are "unmistakable signs of universalization."[5]

4. "Un intento de universalización." José Lezama Lima, "Signs: Outlines of an Anthology," *Orígenes* 9, no. 31 (1952): 65.
5. "De esa manera colaboran en Orígenes, el hombre joven de veinte años, que comienza a intuir la alegría de su expresión, o como George Santayana, desde su centro de Roma, autoriza la inserción en nuestra revista de fragmentos de sus memorias. . . . Por primera vez entre nosotros, lo contemporáneo no era una nostalgia provinciana. . . . En otro de los poemas de Wallace Stevens cita el fragmento de una carta enviada por José Rodríguez Feo. . . . He ahí el detalle, la situación, los impensados agrupamientos, tocando, como arañazo y despertar creadores, la ajena imaginación poética; inequívoco signo de universalización, aparecer en las transmutaciones y misterios imaginativos de otros creadores muy alejados de nuestra latitud y paisaje." Ibid., 66–67. (Thus the young twenty-year-old man, who is beginning to intuit the joy of his expression, and [the older ones] such as George Santayana, who from his center in Rome au-

Although Stevens himself thought this notion of universalization naive and wanted something Cuban to arise from *Orígenes,* it is clear that he envied the group's energies and the creativity involved in forming an autonomous world of art. And even in his direct criticisms of the magazine, he reveals his understanding of their effort at "putting together a world."

> I should like to say a word or two [about] . . . the risk you run in respect to accusations of imperialism. . . . The act of editing a review is a creative act. . . . Assuming that you have a passion for Cuba, you cannot have, or at least you cannot indulge in, a passion for Brinnin and Levin, and so on, at the same time. This is not a question of nationalism, but it is a question of expressing the genius of your country, disengaging it from the mere mass of things, and doing this by means of every poem, every essay, every short story which you publish—every drawing by Mariano. . . . I hope you won't mind my saying this. After all, I am not saying it for your sake, or for the sake of Cuba, but for my own sake. . . . Cuba should be full of Cuban things and not essays on Chaucer. [6 April 1945]

Of course members of the Orígenes Group were not imperialists. José and his friends bitterly criticized the negating influence of the United States. *Orígenes,* wrote Vitier, strengthened Cuban art at a time when Cuban artists were in danger of being overwhelmed by the most powerful nation in the hemisphere.[6]

---

thorizes the insertion of fragments of his memoirs in our journal, collaborate together. . . . For the first time among us, the contemporary is not a provincial nostalgia. . . . In another of the poems by Wallace Stevens, [the poet] quotes a fragment of a letter sent to him by José Rodríguez Feo. . . . There the details, the [heretofore] unthought-of groupings, touch, like a creative pricking and awakening, the far-off poetic imagination; [an] unmistakable sign of universalization appears unexpectedly in the transmutations and mysterious imaginings of other creators far removed from our latitude and landscape.)

6. "Helar nuestras mejores esencias (aquellas que por el contrario Europa nos ayuda a partear y definir), desde la nación más poderosa de este mismo hemisferio." Cintio Vitier, "Ten Cuban Poets," *Orígenes* 5, no. 18 (Summer 1948): 41.

Between 1947 and 1949 José spent most of four semesters at Princeton, preparing to take a Ph.D. in Spanish literature; though he continued to help arrange each number of *Orígenes* from a distance, he eventually agreed with Vitier that his "best essences" would freeze in New Jersey. His mother's recurring instability sharpened the feeling that he must not remain at Princeton. Life in the academy was becoming "academic" and his response to it "anemic," two qualities readers of his letters will not ascribe to him. Soon after *Orígenes* ceased, he took up another project, *Ciclón,* which he published unassisted for nearly three years until 1957. He then traveled extensively in Europe and South America, returning home soon after hearing of Fidel Castro's victory in 1959. He has since published with several Cuban presses, editing, selecting, and writing introductions to collections of stories and essays (including those of his old friend, Henríquez Ureña). He has published translations of a wide range of books, including George Thomson's *Marxism and Poetry,* Mor Jokai's *Black Diamonds,* and the Nigerian Amos Tutola's *The Palm-Wine Drinkard.* One finds him today, at the Union of Artists and Writers in Havana, still very much the man Stevens knew, a tireless reader and correspondent, turning an engaging anecdote on a critical point, an enthusiast who shrinks nevertheless from easy optimism.

The letters between these two very different literary figures tell their own story of the younger man's ability to draw out the more reserved and, on the face of it, less human and generous poet. In fact, he was so successful in doing this that his direct experience with the man was different from most. José and Stevens eventually met in New York after two and a half years of correspondence and then irregularly until a few years before Stevens died. Recalling those rare meetings, José has said, "Stevens was very human indeed and very warm to me and not remote."[7] But José was almost alone in sensing that to know Stevens personally was to know his poetry and vice versa. His unusual but absolute claim to having befriended Stevens is bound up in his knowledge of both the man and his work:

7. Letter from José to Alan Filreis, 26 April 1983.

> He was a very strange combination of a poet who, on one side,
> was very intellectual, very rigorous, and at the same time he
> had this other thing that doesn't go often with the rigorous
> intellectual poet, of this playfulness, a fanciful, fantastic sort of
> vein in him. . . . That was in his personality when you talked
> to him, this playfulness in words.[8]

Stevens' acquaintances tell of his typical remoteness even as
critics complain of the same quality in his poems. But to dip at any
point into their correspondence, and to see the particular kind of
attention Stevens gave to this playful side, encourages us to reassess
his character. José, of course, could not have known that so many
people in Stevens' daily life found him difficult, taciturn, and unre-
sponsive to the subtleties of human interchange. But he did know
and was troubled by the ways in which this opinion of the man's
poetry emerged—Stevens was apparently impervious to life (to bor-
row Edmund Wilson's phrase). In answer to José's second letter
(13 January 1945), Stevens told him that he did not bother to read
one such critic, Yvor Winters, whose already famous essay, "The
Hedonist's Progress," had, in particular, caused José to deplore all
of American criticism. And it is against this background that the
fullest understanding of the most important poem of their friendship, "A Word with José Rodríguez-Feo," comes about.

The letter that prompted the poem was only the third letter José
had written Stevens. But Stevens already knew for certain that the
Cuban's unselfconscious exuberance would be the rule and not the
exception of his style. Since Stevens saved almost all the letters he
received from literary friends, we know that none of them wrote to
him in this informal, if not completely unorganized, fashion. José
tosses into one paragraph staccato questions—about Stevens' concept
of "major man," about John Malcolm Brinnin, about Robert Penn
Warren, about some critic calling Stevens "the Whistler of American poetry." One could attempt any number of times yet never
come close to guessing what combination of bits Stevens would put
together in formulating a reply. Somehow between José's praise for
Stevens' sense of the tropical milieu, his despairing view of Hem-

8. Interview with Peter Brazeau, *Parts of a World,* 143.

ingway's obsessions with "virile problems," and his scrawled post-script questioning the "grotesque" in Spanish tradition, Stevens found a great deal to respond to. We quote José's letter in full here to show how Stevens gave it what we would call a close reading, discovering ironic grist for his poem-reply:

La Habana
Feb. 13, 1945

My dear Mr. Wallace Stevens:

It was grand to hear from you again and to know that those water-colors are cheering your rather gloomy house. I was surprised to learn that your visit to Cuba was of twenty years ago, for your poetry always has had for me a certain evocation of tropical light and colors which I find quite charming and most unusual. Of course, you know that Hemingway has lived among us for a long time; but I have always maintained that the milieu has not affected him at all. I cannot see how anybody could not be impressed by certain *things* which I find completely absent in his most "Spanishied" works. Of course, I have never quite come to admire Hemingway: I mean that if you are a real blood and bone Latino, you find absurd and a bit of an affectation those "virile problems" which seem to bother him so very much. I sincerely think him an Illinois Puritan hunting for exotic sensations in the places and things which are naturally empty of all possibilities of adventure. I should not have said PURITAN because he is really more of a bourgeois and his dislike of certain authors condemns him in my eyes. The fact that he has had such a success makes me fear for that hierarchy of values which must reign in a nation if its culture is not going to fall into the most slappiest of arrange-ments. You are dead right, as you Americans would put it, about Winters. Q: What about Mr. Yarmolinsky's book about Modern Poetry?

You will pardon my stupidity but I don't quite get what you mean by "major men." What do you mean by some "arbitrary object of belief"? I think it was more exact to call them "a source of poetry," but that too is rather ambiguous, eh? Is the intention mythological at all? Why do critics insist in calling

you the Whistler of Amer. poetry? What do you think of Brinnin's poetry and Penn Warren?

I am very grateful for the promised volume of poetry. I will
have all your poems here with me then. Are you ever returning to our lovely Habana?

Yours modestly,
José

[A handwritten note up the left margin reads as follows:]
About Hemingway—Picasso's "Guernica" and Dali's mystifying stories are Sp[anish] treatments of the same subject[,] not
Romantic but macabre[,] in the tradition of Goya in the case
of Guernica—Hemingway has not exploited the grotesque in
our lives. Who has?

Stevens' poem-reply was swift and public; it was sent to *Voices*
within a week along with four other poems. It was also sent to José,
the only reader who would hear its comically private message:

A Word with José Rodríguez-Feo

As one of the secretaries of the moon,
The queen of ignorance, you have deplored
How she presides over imbeciles. The night
Makes everything grotesque. Is it because
Night is the nature of man's interior world?
Is lunar Habana the Cuba of the self?

We must enter boldly that interior world
To pick up relaxations of the known.
For example, this old man selling oranges
Sleeps by his basket. He snores. His bloated breath
Bursts back. What not quite realized transit
Of ideas moves wrinkled in a motion like

The cry of an embryo? The spirit tires,
It has, long since, grown tired, of such ideas.
It says there is an absolute grotesque.
There is a nature that is grotesque within
The boulevards of the generals. Why should
We say that it is man's interior world

Or seeing the spent, unconscious shapes of night,
Pretend they are shapes of another consciousness?
The grotesque is not a visitation. It is
Not apparition but appearance, part
Of that simplified geography, in which
The sun comes up like news from Africa.
    (*CP*, 333–34)

The first two stanzas of this poem are extremely difficult because
of their indirect references. By way of an embarrassed "Thank you,"
José chose to express his regret that the poem was not for *Orígenes*
rather than show his appreciation for its being a special "word" for
him. Perhaps, ironically, he had as much trouble understanding it
as anyone else, although Stevens offered him a little help: "The
point of the poem . . . is that, although the grotesque has taken
possession of the sub-conscious, that is not because there is any particular relationship between the two things" [26 February 1945].
Going on this alone, it would seem that Stevens missed entirely the
point of José's postscript, which had not tried to make a case at all
for the relationship between the grotesque and the subconscious.
But since a full reading of the poem releases more than is accounted
for by Stevens' flat statement, it is hardly surprising to find that it
releases considerably more than is accounted for by José's letter.

Readers of the canon might be reminded of the instructional
thrust of "A High-Toned Old Christian Woman," in which a
speaker defines certain concepts and even specific words for the ad-
dressee. The play in the title of this later poem of instruction cuts
across the idiomatic ("I would like to have a word with José") to
the literal ("I would like to take up a *particular* word—the grotesque—with him"). Taking a cue here, one might best paraphrase
the difficult turns in the opening stanzas by thinking of the entire
poem as something of a "Dear José" letter:

> "Dear José" (one of the secret-keepers of the moon, one who
> acknowledges her reign over the ignorant, but deplores her for
> not drawing the line at imbeciles):
>   I would have a word with you about the word "grotesque."
> You have asked why the moon makes everything grotesque;
> you have wondered if this is because there are special *prov-*

inces for certain experiences. Night, for instance, seems the special province of man's interior world. And night in the tropics, particularly, seems a special portal to that world (cf. "Cuba": a Roman household goddess who escorts children into the world of sleep).

In the second stanza, Stevens seems to go along with these assumptions and joins José's bold entrance into that inner world in order to discover the special "relaxations" of the known world that are best discovered there—in the grotesque aspects, say, of an old man asleep, his bloated breath bursting back. Do such figures suggest more difficult questions: What inchoate beginnings of ideas come to us through these relaxations, these distortions; what unpacked ideas cry out from that which is not quite born to conscious experience?

At this point the poem takes a turn and rejects both the rhetoric and the sentiment involved in the first two stanzas, as if Stevens were suddenly saying, "Forgive me, José, but the dump is full of such ideas." The spirit eventually tires when the once new questions start to sound rhetorical. In response the spirit begins to simplify. And here Stevens becomes as lucid as he was previously convoluted (in lines 11 and 12). The spirit begins to say that everything is grotesque, even something as ordinary and as signposted as the boulevards in Havana (named after generals).

Stevens ends by substituting for José's questions one of his own: Why should we assume that there is a special province for the grotesque? The grotesque is not a visitation from some other world. The grotesque is appearance itself—the act of *anything* coming into view. The last image of the poem is right out of Emily Dickinson. Perhaps Stevens is reminding José of this nontropical poet whose sharply honed sense of the grotesque often worked itself out in "the sun com[ing] up like news from Africa."[9]

But beyond the immediate sense of the grotesque, "A Word with José Rodríguez-Feo" is a reminder of the general difficulties attending those who would like to call themselves keepers and servants of the arts. Yvor Winters is one of the secretaries too. But Winters,

9. See a similar corrective to José's criticism of Hemingway as a poet in Stevens' letter of 26 November 1945.

because of his notion of the special provinces of poetry, deplored Wallace Stevens. Stevens had warned José two weeks earlier of the essential error likely to plague the Yvor Winterses of the world: "Most critics very soon become identified with a group of principles or, say, a group of ideas." The subrosa message of the poem is very nearly the same: never let your ideas get fixed or associated in permanent groupings. Stevens' rather flat statement about the poem, that there is not a particular relationship between the subconscious and the grotesque despite their modern association, has more resonance than is immediately apparent; for Stevens, there should never be any particular relationship between things. All such relationships are fictions that suffice for a time. But poetry, or the *supreme* fiction, most often comes about just as things are no longer sufficing. Those, dear José, are the moments we must record.

If "A Word with José Rodríguez-Feo" allowed Stevens to take issue with the matter of special provinces, the letters themselves continued to call forth lunar images that delineate sharply the writers' awareness of their separate climates: The moon over Havana and the moon over Connecticut were different creatures. For a time the men treated North and South as simple opposites and playfully traded envies: Stevens' "I am always chummy with anyone named José or Pepe" for José's "I would like to have an Anglo-Saxon about to discover or re-discover our wonders." José noted that "someday someone must write an opus on the effects of climate on the imagination." Such a conclusion made him one of the first of Stevens' critics to suggest how much could be made of this in his poetry [21 September 1948]. And when it came to the more subtle aspects of their North/South consciousnesses, José proved to have more independent and discriminating ideas than Stevens could ever have hoped for in a correspondent, friend, or critic.

José's affinity with George Santayana's insights into matters North and South revived Stevens' interest in Santayana after four decades. The important sonnet exchange of 1899—Stevens' "Cathedrals Are Not Built along the Sea," delivered one night to his mentor's room and prompting Santayana's reply, "Cathedrals by the Sea"—was long past and relegated for the most part to memories of undergraduate days at Harvard. The quatrain Stevens published in the *Harvard Advocate* a few days after his final evenings in Santayana's rooms was written as a farewell.[10] Indeed, after a brief attempt at a writing career in New York, Stevens said farewell to the pure, aesthetic life Santayana had briefly held out to him. Now, forty-five years later, when José put into Stevens' hands a letter to the Cuban from Santayana himself, there was a particular sentiment in that note which exhilarated the mature Stevens: Santayana's line, "I have always, somewhat sadly, bowed to expediency or fate." We can only speculate on the extent of Stevens' identification with this notion and what he made of it. He quoted it to others. More to the point, however, is the way in which his second major poem written expressly for José explores his own sense of his paradoxically chosen fate:

> The Novel
>
> The crows are flying above the foyer of summer.
> The winds batter it. The water curls. The leaves
> Return to their original illusion.
>
> The sun stands like a Spaniard as he departs,
> Stepping from the foyer of summer into that
> Of the past, the rodomontadean emptiness.
>
> *Mother was afraid I should freeze in the Parisian hotels.*
> *She had heard of the fate of an Argentine writer. At*
>   *night,*
> *He would go to bed, cover himself with blankets—*
>
> *Protruding from the pile of wool, a hand,*
> *In a black glove, holds a novel by Camus. She begged*
> *That I stay away.* These are the words of José . . .
>
> He is sitting by the fidgets of a fire,
> The first red of red winter, winter-red,
> The late, least foyer in a qualm of cold.
>
> How tranquil it was at vividest Varadero,
> While the water kept running through the mouth of
>   the speaker
> Saying: *Olalla blanca in el blanco,*

10. He sought the music of the distant spheres
       By night, upon an empty plain, apart;
    Nor knew they hid their singing all the years
       Within the keeping of his human heart.

Lol-lolling the endlessness of poetry.
But here tranquility is what one thinks.
The fire burns as the novel taught it how.

The mirror melts and moulds itself and moves
And catches from nowhere brightly-burning breath.
It blows a glassy brightness on the fire

And makes the flame flame that makes it bite the wood
And bite the hard-bite, barking as it bites.
The arrangement of the chairs is so and so,

Not as one would have arranged them for oneself,
But in the style of the novel, its tracing
Of an unfamiliar in the familiar room,

A *retrato* that is strong because it is like,
A second that grows first, a black unreal
In which a real lies hidden and alive.

Day's arches are crumbling into the autumn night.
The fire falls a little and the book is done.
The stillness is the stillness of the mind.

Slowly the room grows dark. It is odd about
That Argentine. Only the real can be
Unreal today, be hidden and alive.

It is odd, too, how that Argentine is oneself,
Feeling the fear that creeps beneath the wool,
Lies on the breast and pierces into the heart,

Straight from the Arcadian imagination,
Its being beating heavily in the veins,
Its knowledge cold within one as one's own;

And one trembles to be so understood and, at last,
To understand, as if to know became
The fatality of seeing things too well.
(*CP,* 457–59)

What we have here is not a portrait of José but of Stevens' idealized view of himself imposed on José even as he imposes the same
view on Santayana, retired since 1932 to a convent room in Rome.
There, as in Stevens' room in Hartford, "tranquility is what one

thinks"; there things are arranged "not as one would have arranged them for oneself," but as "the *fatality* of seeing" dictates. The poem is confusing only insofar as Stevens suggests but does not resolve his and Santayana's preference of the quotidian to the marvelous, the still to the active. José's letter of 21 September 1948, which contains the source for the poem's italicized anecdote about his mother's fear over her son's plans to move to Paris, discloses Stevens' use of far more than the mere anecdote José gave him permission to quote. In his letter containing the anecdote, José, describing himself as caught in a room with books, dreaming of Varadero Beach, muses yet again on what positive effects his southern climate would have on Stevens if he would relent and come for a visit. But in "The Novel" Stevens responds with the consolations of afternoons and evenings in a room, a dominant image in poems of this period. The señora's unfounded and awkward fear that, like the younger Argentine expatriate she'd heard of, her son would go to Paris and die with a book in his hand while aspiring to a place among European literati reminded Stevens of his own position in a warm, well-lighted room. The hearth fire by the comfortable novel-reader in the poem is warmer for the fact that Stevens never committed the mistake of the Argentine, never succumbed to the lures of expatriate American modernism as a social, even economic fact. As he had written years before, prophetic of this poem, "My job is not now with poets from Paris. It is to keep the fire-place burning."[11] So he may retire to a room safe from the freezing cold feared by the señora. Indeed the fire burns out of control in several middle stanzas—melting the mirror, catching "from nowhere the [young man's] brightly-burning breath." Once the breath itself catches fire, it in turn "makes flame flame and makes it bite the blood/And bite the hard-bite, barking as it bites." This conflagration occurs, apparently, while the man of the poem is actually reading, for soon "the fire falls a little and the book is done."

How could the real José interpret this as other than Stevens' message to him of his preference for a still life of thought and books over accounts of people, activities, and places? José had been sharply warned against letting his letters lapse into reports of his

11. Letter to William Carlos Williams, 14 October 1925, *L,* 246.

reading; however, he would not have been surprised at Stevens' confession to his bookdealer in Paris that he lived "in a Paris that has never existed and that is composed of things other people have said," a Paris "that may be wholly fiction, but, if so . . . is a precious fiction."[12]

What was required of José, therefore, was a considerable degree of independence when it came to making sense of certain ambiguous aspects of Stevens' avowed aesthetic values. José knew, for example, that the terms "North" and "South" carried enormous emotional weight in Santayana's thought. Santayana associated the North with its barren Protestantism, which had become for him the comprehensive symbol of all that was grievously wrong with the business of modern life. As opposed to the South, where form, cultural pessimism, strong authority, and beauty for its own sake were admired, the North held a disregard for form, taught its children unthinking optimism, and provided no strong cultural or personal authority. The letters in this present volume, which for several years amount to a protracted argument between North and South, have Santayana very much as their source. Anyone who has read *Harmonium* (1923) and *Ideas of Order* (1935) as closely as José did has noticed Stevens' emphasis on the South as a place that nourishes the imagination and the North as one that counteracts it. Until 1940 Florida had offered Stevens an actual escape. Now, while justifying it in a number of ways after beginning his correspondence with José, Stevens chose to remain in his impoverished North where, as José bitterly observed from his own experience and his close reading of Santayana, all doors opened on routine, enterprise, strict if unhappy monogamy, and a life of dull repetitive work.

Drawn to poetic subtlety and pious retreat, any of these three men, if caught in the North, would either fold up his heart or flee to the Catholic extremities. José and Santayana both fled. Stevens, it would seem, folded up his heart. The sixty-six-year-old José Rodríguez Feo is perhaps one of the very few of Stevens' surviving friends to find unsurprising the poet's reputed conversion to Catholicism, a gesture that would suggest the end of a full swing away from Santayana's aesthetic orthodoxy and back to it. At the time he

12. Letter to Paule Vidal, 2 April 1953, *L*, 773.

wrote to Stevens, José persisted in finding in Santayana a language
of northern and southern aestheticism in relation to Stevens' poems,
which likewise helped him find his own way in breaking through
at least some of Stevens' carefully guarded defenses.

One way was to write an essay himself for *Orígenes* on Santayana's role as a cultural critic. There José notes that Santayana "did
not cease enriching himself with the conflict he had to confront by
situating himself between two essentially opposing cultures: Spanish Catholicism and American Puritanism."[13] Having spent enough
years in the North to appreciate what he emphasized as "the meaning of [Santayana's] work as a criticism of modern American conscience,"[14] José wrote sympathetically of Santayana's predicament
and ultimate choice. Stevens' reaction to the bitter criticism Santayana aimed at America is more complex than José's, in part because
Stevens could claim no native southern setting and because he had
chosen *The* Hartford ("Year in and year out you'll do well with
The Hartford")—a comic extension of all that Santayana deplored.
Now an old man, aware that Santayana's seclusion in a room was
like his own in an upstairs bedroom, Stevens would naturally be
drawn to the notion that one bows, with dignity, to expediency or
fate. As Stevens increasingly retreated into solitude, he identified
with Santayana on his own terms. Though he was reluctant to
admit to José this particular association with Santayana—if only to
give credence to his advice about turning outdoors for one's health—
Stevens' late portrait of the Spaniard in his monastic room in "To
an Old Philosopher in Rome" (1952) strongly suggests that he did
equate his own closed doors with a proper bowing.

Himself the author of a revealing prose-poem entitled "The
Closed Door," José did not misinterpret Stevens' comment about his
life, in which he habitually "shut the door" to his own private bedroom in the very middle of the demands of family life [27 December 1951]. Whatever Stevens felt about Santayana's retreat to a

13. "No por eso dejó de enriquecerse con el conflicto que tuvo que
afrontar al situarse entre dos culturas escencialmente opuesta: la Católica
española y la Puritana americana." José Rodríguez Feo, "George Santayana: Critic of a Culture," *Orígenes* 1, no. 1 (Spring 1944): 37–38.
14. "La significacion de la obra como critica de la consciencia moderna
americana." Ibid., 36–37.

convent, he gave José the impression that his life, especially at
home, was similarly bound up, that he had closed the door on
everyone, that he was, indeed, José's "Dear Prisoner of Hartford."
In "To an Old Philosopher in Rome," Santayana's convent, his
Lebensraum, is also Stevens' own room: the three of them lived
essential portions of their lives "beneath the shadow of a shape / In
a confusion of bed and books" (*CP,* 508). José's "Closed Door" is
an answer to, and probably a conscious imitation of, the vivid repre-
sentation of Cuban color Stevens had guessed at in his poem about
the San Miguel resort. Indeed, with little control whatever, José's
piece wildly outcolors Stevens'. After an absence the narrator of the
prose-poem returns to his room at San Miguel and faces the major
choice of his life in such a naturally inspiring place: Should he turn
inward to think on it or outward to live in it? José answers the
question indirectly: "In that empty room . . . everything corrobo-
rated the adhesion to the tedious."[15] When José was drawn away
again to begin graduate study at Princeton a year later, he wrote
Stevens that coming north had *"closed the door* on many thoughts
which assail and make me unhappy. It makes for a sedentary life.
It has the tendency of making us . . . forget the passionate side of
life. How can we cultivate the passions at Princeton. They dry up
here. . . . Here one must not show one's emotions or else people
give you a puzzled glance" [15 November 1948].

   In Stevens' attempt to answer such a question, his relationship
with José changed. As for the younger man, his view of Stevens
was to become much more complicated before it became clearer.

   For the period beginning September 1947, José attained a resident visa and realized that he could remain permanently in the
United States if he so chose. He studied with Don Amerigo Castro
(1885–1972), the great scholar of sixteenth-century Spanish literature, whose geo-cultural theories served to heighten Santayana's
main lesson about the boundaries between North and South. (In
one of his books, Castro explained the positive effect of Arab and
Moor cultures on the art and life of Europeanized Spain.) Particularly because Castro's celebrated presence at Princeton justified it,

   15. "En aquella sala vacía . . . [t]odo corroboraba la adhesión al
tedio." José Rodríguez Feo, "The Closed Door," *Orígenes* 3, no. 2 (Fall
1946): 21.

studying "southern" literature at a prominent northern institution may not have bothered José, though he increasingly sensed something was unnatural. He expressed it vaguely, we might say in Stevensean terms: "That savage, tropical light [in Cuba] seems here a little too glaring" [15 November 1948].

It was not until winter that José's loneliness peaked. After being snowbound for several days in "the Great Storm" that crippled the Northeast in the winter of 1947–48, he wrote to Stevens for the first time about his fatherlessness. By the manner in which he began his lament with references to Stevens' own sadness, the older man could tell that the younger needed parental authority as much as friendship. From Cuba in 1946, José had written that he was "as lonely as ever and quite happy in my isolation." But in Princeton, where passions dried up, Stevens' letters provided human contact and no less than a reason for living. "Without them," José wrote, "I feel a bit destitute and like giving up the whole farce." Now there was great pressure on Stevens to offer an older adult's advice on how one endures life. But these pressures tended to expose his own ambivalence.

With his daughter, Stevens had adopted the model of his father's letters to him at Harvard, which were regular, prodding, almost entirely practical, and attached to bank checks. Letters to Holly at Vassar, 1941–42, were so practical that they were exasperating to her—cautious and never overinvolved. These letters utterly failed to send the message that one should stay in college and apply oneself. Indeed, Holly rejected her father's practical advice just as Stevens had succumbed to Garrett Barcalow Stevens'. To her father's shock and dismay, Holly left Vassar after a month of her sophomore year, feeling purposeless as a student after Pearl Harbor. She wrote home that she intended to work despite Stevens' insistence that "you don't find yourself on your way through life by getting a job" (*L*, 426). For many months, indeed several years, the Stevens house on Westerly Terrace was even quieter and emptier than it had been, and Stevens admitted feeling like a failure as a father.

Unaware of his timing, José put straightforwardly his need for Stevens' guidance; he confessed his loneliness in faintly suicidal language which surely gave Stevens pause as he gathered up what paternal skills he still trusted for further attempts at advice. And here again Santayana provides a key. When Stevens identifies his own "disillusioned aestheticism"[16] explicitly in Santayana's terms in poems, letters, and lectures of this period, the analogy is to a house that is empty, a husband and wife unhappy, a family disunited. In "Two or Three Ideas" (1951), for example, Stevens remarks that Santayana's thesis that God is dead and needs replacing has left us "feeling dispossessed and alone in a solitude, like children without parents, in a home that seem[s] deserted, in which the amical rooms and halls [have] taken on a look of hardness and emptiness" (*OP*, 208). It is as if the acceptance of Santayana's thesis, as opposed to the conventional American one offered by his own father, meant a serious questioning of at least the broader implications of family, home, job, and security.

But Stevens' other response to José is surprisingly authoritarian and parental. When writing to allay the young man's fears of uselessness—for even his more or less permanent return to Cuba by 1949 did not, of course, immediately relieve José's anxieties— Stevens will reject the aesthetic life in details so delicious as to be almost transparently overstated. Even stronger, however, is his expression of the values of Hartford he had inherited as an American son; astoundingly, he talks of the time when José will outgrow his aestheticism, marry, and get a regular job—a set of North American conventions obviously beyond José's psychological framework.

During this period Stevens doubled his efforts in encouraging José to report to him the Cuban anecdotes and scenes that made his friend's life seem less literary and more real. We have seen the effect of the anecdote that became "The Novel." Stevens loved even more José's nonliterary discussion of the kidnapping of the family Great Dane, Linda, and the tales of his mother's vengeful neighbor, Consuelo. "Literature nowadays is largely about nothing by nobodies," he wrote. "Is it not so? What kind of book would that dazzling human animal Consuelo sit down to read after she had finished washing the blood off her hands and had hidden once more her machete in the piano?" [1 December 1948].

Likewise, when it came to responding to José's dismay at critical

16. A phrase from John Gould Fletcher's review of *Harmonium*, "The Revival of Aestheticism," *Freeman* 8 (19 December 1923).

attacks aimed at Stevens' poetry, Stevens tended to reassure by not very subtly falling back on the position of the practical, Protestant father. "There is something about poets . . . that make them . . . easily and violently disturbed by hostile comment. Among other men not of their sort, *as for example, business men* . . . having to deal with the same sort of thing, it would not receive a moment's attention" [26 January 1945]. Here Stevens indeed disassociates himself from his young Cuban friend. To get a job, he suggests, to live my American life, is to be able to repress criticism and still celebrate praise. This kind of attitude weaves itself in and out of his numerous admissions of his healthy envy of a life of literature and leisure and his basic resemblance to José.

Stevens' fatherly sermons on the subject of his preference for life over literature are genuine. He was tired of penetratingly sympathetic criticism, even José's, on the significance of the role of the imagination in his poetry and he could react quite harshly to anything that smacked of literariness in José's letters. We can even imagine how the wording of these oddly bitter reactions to José's life of books might have begun to gall the younger man: "What I really like to have from you is not your tears on the death of Bernanos, but news about chickens raised on red peppers and homesick rhapsodies of the Sienese look of far away Havana and news about people I don't know, who are more fascinating to me than all the characters in all the novels of Spain, which I am unable to read" [25 October 1948]. By now this American poet has protested too much. José knows full well that Stevens would have loved to read all the books of Spain. Stevens' notion of the proper description of Havana is itself derivative. Far less adventurous than his Cuban friend, he could be assuaged by "the *Sienese* look of far away Havana,"—he who knows even less of Italy than Cuba. Yet he continually chides José for living out of books: "Intellectual isolation loses value in an existence of books. I think I sent you some time ago a quotation from Henry James about living in a world of creation." Indeed Stevens had quoted James to José back in 1945, but as we might suspect, Stevens' James is not at all clear on the issue of choosing real over imagined acts: " 'To live *in* the world of creation—to get into it and stay in it—to frequent it and haunt it— to *think* intensely and fruitfully—to woo combinations and inspira-

tions into being by a depth and continuity of attention and meditation—this is the only thing' " [20 June 1945]. Here Stevens assumes
in James a choice of creative thinking as a way of living in the
world. However, on the subject of Henry James generally, as with
Santayana, José was not easily led into a single interpretation. He
knew James' fiction as well or better than Stevens did, having
studied the novels for a senior thesis at Harvard and re-read many
of them since. José's approach to this issue was to clarify the role of
James' narrator as a man of frustrated passion cut off from the actuality of life. In one of his letters from Princeton about the sexlessness of life there, he emphasized his point by referring to James and
the fate of bachelors. What the inexperienced, unmarriable narrator-
critic of "The Figure in the Carpet" will never know is physical
love; to unravel its mysteries he looks in vain not in others' beds but
in all the books of a famous writer, yet is left feeling, unsatisfac-
torily, as if he *had* looked into others' beds. "I don't know if I, a
born spectator in a fashion," José wrote, "will assemble all the bits
and ends . . . and weave a similarly odd figure in the carpet, ever."
James left America, José notes, because in cultures where passion
was tolerated or envied, where a spectator's knowledge could form
an elegant artifice, James' "limited imagination" could bear fruit
and be true to life [January 1948]. That is to say, for José there was
a place—possibly Cuba but certainly not America—where literature
alone could satisfy and teach one about life, especially the man who
did not or could not know life continuously or directly.

It is ironic that an older, increasingly reticent Stevens felt it his
place to persuade José to leave his world of books and live all he
could while he could—no less ironic, at any rate, than Lambert
Strether's similar insistence to *his* young friend. It is doubly ironic,
then, that in order to persuade José, Stevens frequently sent him
titles to read on the subject. On one occasion Stevens sent a short
story by V. S. Pritchett about a man who uses fiction as a way of
living. From Stevens' own description of the man in the story, José
may well have been reminded of Stevens himself, who admitted to
living in places that don't exist and are made out of words, "composed of the things other people have said" of them. But a parental
Stevens saw no hypocrisy in making his point perfectly clear to
José: "I sent [Pritchett's story] to you because you are becoming so

literary that you ought to understand that life fights back and that it will get you even on the top floor of the Peacock Inn if you are not careful" [22 January 1948].

No matter how hard he tried to qualify his love of literature, in doing so José incessantly reminded Stevens of other books he might enjoy reading. It was a tricky business. Eight years of letter writing had taught him that Stevens was as likely to follow up a literary reference as to ignore or disparage it. By 1952 José was writing about life to please Stevens even as Stevens doggedly interpreted this to mean that his young friend was suggesting more books to read. When writing from a hospital bed where he was recovering from a pancreatic illness, where days were temporarily limited to what one could find to read, still José wrote insistently about life: events in Cuba, politics, how useless it is for New York City to prepare for a nuclear attack. Thus he must have been annoyed when, soon after, Stevens overresponded to a title suggested earlier, a book of profiles by the French critic Marcel Schwob, *Vies Imaginaires* (1896). After reading a few chapters Stevens wrote to dismiss José's choice as "definitely effete." Reading Schwob would never amount to much for him since his own interest, he said, was not "in *pure literature* of that type" [19 February 1952]. This quick dismissal of Schwob and strongly implied criticism of José's tastes bothered the young man so much that he wrote an essay-length retort the day he received Stevens' letter and attempted for the first time to point out the hypocrisy of Stevens' life.

In this letter of 25 February 1952, José attacks Stevens' notion of "pure literature," uses a detailed, negative comparison with André Gide to reclaim Schwob, exposes Stevens' love of the South as misled and contradictory, restates his own impatience with the literary history of Protestantism, and then confronts Stevens in language found nowhere else in letters anyone dared write Stevens: "You say I am deeply set in literature. But I find no difference between what I read and what I live," he wrote. What had bound them now distinguished them. "I think a man from your latitude has other intentions when he picks up a book."

To this critical letter, Stevens did not reply. Weeks, then months went by—still no letter between them. Four months later almost to the day, José, not without some trepidation to be sure, left a message for Stevens that he would very soon arrive in the United States. By this time, June 1952, Stevens had begun corresponding with another young man, Peter Lee, a Korean poet who spent some time at Yale—a man, a boy really, younger than José when he first wrote Stevens. The day after José wrote his critical letter from Havana in February, Peter Lee had introduced himself to Stevens by making a gift of a Korean scroll. Like José, Peter Lee was the son Stevens never had, the scholar and the temporary expatriate he never was. Like José, Peter sent Stevens the artifacts of his culture, which elated Stevens. To match Mariano's painting of the pineapple, there was now on Stevens' bedroom wall the oriental scroll. Just as Stevens once wrote that he simply liked to write letters to people named José or Pepe, so he responded to Lee as a foreigner, one who was as removed from Hartford as anyone could have been: "Dear Peter, or possibly Pierre," he began a later letter, "I love all this scholar's life you lead" (L, 839). When it became clear that the two had solitude in common, Stevens wrote to Peter exactly as he had to José: "More than anything else [Lee's last note from Paris] made me understand how much a Korean student, or, if you like, a young Korean scholar and a somewhat old American student who never had time to become a scholar resemble each other. I wanted all my life to go to Paris" (L, 845).

Eventually, it would seem, all these hyperliterate young men were alike; the pattern—elation at the news of a new letter writer, followed by sympathy, then identity, then increasingly organized criticism of the literary life—repeats itself exactly in the case of Peter Lee. By the early 1950s Stevens no longer had José's descriptions of his mother's goats, mules, dogs, and nosy neighbors, but he had Peter Lee's. He wrote to Norman Holmes Pearson to tell him the joy Peter's letters gave him, just as he had to James Guthrie and Barbara Church about José: "Recently I got a letter from [Peter] in which he described the square in Fribourg opposite the post office as full of country people selling butter and vegetables, chickens and eggs, and, in addition, he described the town itself as full of school girls not only from this country but from various parts of Europe, not to speak of Egypt." But a few days after receiving this letter from Peter, that Sunday to be exact, Stevens was glancing through Mallarmé at home and discovered that a sentence Lee used at the end of his letter about the country people and alluring school girls, which Stevens had taken as a sign of the young man's vigor and normalcy, had been plagiarized directly from Mallarmé. "Peter lives a great deal out of books," he concluded sadly to Pearson. "I suppose . . . that the butter and vegetables and chickens and eggs were all artificial and that the school girls, especially the dark-eyed jewels from Cairo, were just wax stuffed with sawdust" (L, 871–72). By now the disappointed New England father in him denied the younger Latin self affirmed by José, whose letters are so much more appealing and truer to life than Peter's. Stevens responded to statements of the hypersensitive *origenista* by being ambivalent, by condemning the meditative life in the same breath with which he admitted his attraction to it. Now, to Lee, he announced his discontent with the boy who would plagiarize literature to enhance life and lectured with a moralism he never used to argue the same point with José.

> Dear Peter:
> . . . It is unnatural to think of men who have *grown venerable in asceticism* and meditation as plump babies. . . . Enfin, I refuse to take seriously the idea that living in a bamboo grove increases one's heft. . . . Anyhow, a man whose life is devoted to the study of poetry is as fully a specialist as a man whose life is spent in an effort to find a way of changing sea water into champagne. (L, 873; emphasis added)

Following José's letter of 25 February 1952, the correspondence between José and Stevens was not quite finished, but after a few more long letters it fell off quickly and was increasingly taken up with small talk. Their relationship had radically changed since the summer of 1946, when the Cuban could not quite track Stevens down. José arrived in New York in June 1952. Getting his message, Stevens wrote: "Why don't you . . . stop over here for lunch some day? Nothing would make me happier than to see you" [30 June 1952]. But on Independence Day, writing from the Plaza Hotel on Central Park South, José informed Stevens that he would be unable to meet him on this trip; he was leaving for Havana that very day. When he returned in the autumn, he added, they would have to be sure to get together. But he didn't return that or any autumn and never saw Stevens again. He wrote two more letters and sent a Christmas card. It was obvious to José that he had not changed Stevens as much as he would have liked or had dreamed back in 1944, that Stevens had certainly not taken the cue that he should put aside a monotonous job and go abroad just once to check real against long-imagined things. It must have piqued José's new distaste for Stevens' words of resignation, which now, at the end of their friendship, suggested that some of the time José had been to him less a real than an imagined friend: "I have been working at the office, nothing else: complaining a little about it but content, after all, that I have that solid rock under my feet, and enjoying the routine without minding too much that I have to pay a respectable part of my income to the government in order that someone else . . . may sit at the Cafe X at Aix or go to a lecture at the Sorbonne" [13 January 1953].

ORIGINS

1944–1945

B entre 12 y 14
Rpto. Almendares
Havana
Nov. 30, 1944

My dear Mr. Stevens,

With such ardor one must be allowed the pecadillo of forgetting
that after all there is a due respect to the author. Being almost satisfied with the translations of "Esthétique du Mal," I could have published it in our magazine. But then I recollected Marianne Moore's
words—why don't *you* translate Stevens? Yes, I had already translated some poems from *Harmonium* [and] *Notes Toward a Supreme Fiction.* That was at Harvard and they were too "anglicized."
They had the Spanish polish, the perfect poetic recognition of similar images, combinations, and the affinities which make it so difficult
to keep the poem from turning into something quite foreign.

I like very much to send you *Orígenes,* our review. And W. C.
Williams could tell you of my virtuosity, I mean my ability as translator.[1] For you must justly fear. I hope you will write and tell me
you're willing. *Orígenes* would publish "Esthétique" this winter or
spring. Of course, you could select something else or send us a new
poem.

Allow me this opportunity, now, to wish you the happy greetings
for Christmas. And pardon such naïve familiarity. Indeed, I feel I
know you quite well already. And if I have hesitated so long to

1. See Introduction, pp. 6–7.

address you, it is because "this is a part of the sublime from which we shrink."[2]

Yours ever, a most enthusiastic Cuban reader,
José Rodríguez Feo

[Hartford, Connecticut]
December 8, 1944

Dear Mr. Fes [sic]:

Your letter of November 30th gives me more pleasure than I can tell you. I shall be most interested to have you translate the "Esthétique." Unfortunately, my knowledge of Spanish is too limited to make it possible for me to be of the slightest help to you.

Do send me a copy of *Orígenes*. At the present time I subscribe to *Sur* of Buenos Aires, and enjoy reading a few pages of it now and then.[1] I don't know why I should not enjoy reading a page of *Orígenes* just as much.

I am grateful to you for your letter and shall look forward to seeing your translation.

Yours very truly,
Wallace Stevens

[Hartford, Connecticut]
January 4, 1945

Dear Mr. Feo:

Thank you for your very agreeable letter.

If the "Esthétique" is too long, I shall be very glad to have you use something else, as you like.

2. José quotes from the second stanza of the first section of "Esthétique du Mal" (*CP*, 314).

1. Probably the most important South American literary review of the period, *Sur* (Buenos Aires) was edited first by Victoria Ocampo and then Roger Caillois from 1931 to 1954. *Sur* published articles, stories, poems, and reviews by Alfonso Reyes, Jorge Luis Borges, Pedro Henríquez Ureña, Lewis Mumford, Santayana, James Joyce, Leon Chestov, André Breton, Ramon Fernandéz, Jean-Paul Sartre, André Gide. One doubts that Stevens missed the translation earlier that year of his own "Sunday Morning" by Jorge Luis Borges and A. Bioy Cesares in *Sur* 16 (March–April 1944): 98–111. See Stevens' letter to Henry Church, *L*, 418.

The copies of *Orígenes* came yesterday, and I spent last evening reading them. They remind me of *Éventail,* which was published at Geneva about the time of the last war.[1] The fastidious make-up and Mariano's happy little drawings touch me (Mariano is in fact exquisite). Nothing quite so unconcerned has come my way for a long time. Man's fever is not present here.

Of course, for the reader of the exterior, what is of particular interest is the Cubans themselves. I very much wish I could read more exactly the essay of Aníbal Rodríguez on the bases of alegría. His subject is a footnote to felicidad, which, after all, is the great subject. And just as Eric Bentley, in the current *Kenyon Review*[2] says that, today, treatises absorb the attention that novels absorbed twenty years ago, so I think that the philosophical and critical work in *Orígenes* is better than anything else, so far as I am able to judge it. I am quite unable to judge the poetry because of my unfamiliarity with the language, and because in poetry the language is everything.

I doubt if Santayana was any more isolated at Cambridge than he wished to be. While I did not take any of his courses and never heard him lecture, he invited me to come to see him a number of times and, in that way, I came to know him a little. I read several poems to him and he expressed his own view of the subject of them in a sonnet which he sent me, and which is in one of his books.[3] This was forty years ago, when I was a boy and he was not yet in mid-life. Obviously, his mind was full of the great projects of his future and, while some of these have been realized, it is possible to think that many have not. It would be easy to speak of his interest and sympathy; it might amuse you more to know that Sparklets were then something new and that Santayana liked to toy with them as he charged the water which he used to make a highball or two. They seemed to excite him. I always came away from my visits to

1. *Éventail: Revue de littérature & d'art,* published in Geneva, 1917–19.
2. "Kahler and Mumford," *Kenyon Review* 7 (Winter 1945): 143–49.
3. Santayana's "Cathedrals by the Sea: Reply to a Sonnet Beginning 'Cathedrals are not built along the sea,' " in *A Hermit of Carmel and Other Poems* (New York: Scribner's, 1901), 122. Stevens' sonnet, "Cathedrals Are Not Built along the Sea," was published in the *Harvard Monthly* 27 (May 1899): 95 (HS).

him feeling that he made up in the most genuine way for many things that I needed. He was then still definitely a poet.

I should like to continue to receive *Orígenes,* and enclose a check for $5.00. Since you have been kind enough to send me the first three numbers, please apply this as a subscription beginning with Number One. I shall be looking forward to your next number: the Winter number.

Very truly yours,
Wallace Stevens

Habana, Cuba
January 13, [1945]

Dear Mr. Stevens:

I cannot express my delight at being so intimately taken into your recollection of Señor Santayana. It amused me indeed to read about his interest in Sparklets. It comes as a sort of ironic commentary on the pompous, delicious and traditional Cambridge existence; I regard his excitement as a strange and lovely thing. I think you share with him that rediscovery of the supreme beauty that small, every-day objects have for the poetic eye. Another reason for my feeling quite astonished when reading American criticism. I distinctly remember Yvor Winters' essay on your poetry: there he goes around the subject, in a morbid, cowboy-like manner and calls you all sorts of unpleasant things and never sees the target. I mean he misses completely the point: that your poetry, just as Marianne Moore's, is a delicate, elegant, and very human annotation of the small things of life which at bottom makes this our "imperfect paradise" so worthwhile and of course unique. His rendition of "Sunday Morning"[1] is absurd and if a critic as loudly proclaimed as Mr. Winters cannot sum up intelligently the simplest passages, what are we to think, I mean us poor latinos who must some time look here and there for guidance into the more difficult realms of the poetic expression? To whom can I go now? To Mr. [R. P.] Blackmur?[2]

1. "Wallace Stevens, or the Hedonist's Progress," in *The Anatomy of Nonsense* (Norwalk, Conn.: New Directions, 1943), 88–119.
2. José had written to Blackmur six months earlier, praising his work as "an unavoidable guide" through American literature. 10 August 1944, Blackmur Papers, Princeton University Library.

Can you suggest some intelligent creature or some good, solid book on modern American poetry? Or hasn't that book arrived yet?

Your praise of *Orígenes* has pleased me immensely, and you don't know how it has encouraged me—to go on. Thank you for the money. I felt tempted to send it back in return for the following: *Ideas of Order* or *The Man With The Blue Guitar* which I haven't been able to get yet. But I won't be so mercenary or abuse your kindness. Perhaps, I can get these books in New York next summer when I return to the States. By the way, you do not mention the place where your "Academic Discourse in Habana" appeared?[3] Some Cuban poet spoke to me of it a while ago. Is there such a poem? Moreover you didn't tell me when you were here last. I am very happy to see that you have enjoyed Mariano's work. I don't know if you were in New York when the Cuban exhibition opened at the Museum of Modern Art.[4] The pictorial movement here is very interesting. I think it rates second only to that of Mejico.[5] Since you like him so much, I will send you one of his water-colors. But let me tell you: it is a gift so don't be sending any check. You know us Spaniards. I should feel very much hurt. Mariano is now in New York, but when I see him I shall tell him of you and he won't be displeased with the lines you dedicated him in your last letter.

3. It appeared as "Discourse in a Cantina at Havana" in *Revista de avance* 10, no. 40 (15 November 1929): 326–27, and was probably translated by Jorge Mañach. Stevens had a copy of the translation; in 1943 R. P. Blackmur had given a copy of the issue of the Cuban magazine containing the translation to Allen Tate, who forwarded it to Stevens. 6 July 1944, Princeton University manuscript, Tate Papers.

4. "Modern Cuban Painters," an exhibition at the Museum of Modern Art from 16 March through 7 May 1944, included Mariano Rodríguez, René Portocarrero, and Mario Carreño.

5. The "pictorial movement" José mentions here was inspired by Mariano's devotion to the Mexican sculptor Lozano. According to the *Cultural Annual of Cuba* of 1943, Mariano, Portocarrero, and Carreño were principals in a salon called "La Sala de Retorno," roughly translated, "the room of return." Formed in the early 1940s, the group intended to return to various traditional drawings, vignettes, and national religious subjects. Mariano's roosters, bathers, and crucifixions, and Portocarrero's cloth-and-cardboard angels, butterflies, and religious feasts were important examples of the movement. Havana: Dirección General de Relaciones Culturales, 1943, 122–27.

Excuse my ignorance: who are the *major men* so consistently present in your last poems? Do you write verses for occasional frivolities: like On a birthday, To a plate of Boston beans, On the occasion of sending her a lovely lingerie—you know, the sort of light verse some poets have cultivated indeed some great poets like Martial, Mallarmé, and our own Góngora?

Speaking of French poetry, at the moment, I read *A Rebours* where Huysmans compares the decadent poetry of the Romans with that of his own days. It is curious that Nisard called his book *Etudes sur les poètes latins de la décadence.*[6] Do you suppose this volume induced Mallarmé to say:

> J'ai mal à la dent
> d'être décadent.

Alfonso Reyes, the Mexican critic, seems to share my suspicion. And then it is nice to think how the term *decadent* is thrown around these days by some critics, here and over-there.

I must close now. To-morrow I leave for Santiago de Cuba and must get some rest. Let us hope you will write soon and give partial confirmation to the many questions presented above.

> Gratefully yours,
> José Rodríguez-Feo
> (one name, compound)
> (I abhor the *Feo* by itself.)

> [Hartford, Connecticut]
> January 26, 1945

Dear Mr. Rodríguez-Feo:

I put off replying to your letter of January 23d until after the arrival of the watercolors. They came on the coldest day of one of our coldest winters, and they looked unhappy in the gloomy light of that particular day. However, the picture of the pineapples, which I put in my bedroom, is now quite the master of that scene, and is as bright and cheerful a thing as there is in the rest of the house. The other one, I figure, I shall have to take to New York to

6. Désiré Nisard (1806–88) wrote *Etudes de moeurs et de critique sur les poètes latins de la décadence* in 1829.

have framed the next time I go down. They are both a good deal more Cuban than you are likely to realize so that, in addition to one's sense of a new and fresh artist, there is the sense of an unfamiliar place. I say unfamiliar, even though I have been to Havana twice, but the stranger in Havana probably gets very little of Cuba. On my first trip, about 25 years ago I should say, I went down alone and spent the greater part of a week there. Then, about five years later,[1] my wife and I stopped there for about a day on the way to California by way of the Canal. When I was there alone, on my first trip, I walked round the town a great deal and concluded by wanting in the wildest way to study Spanish, which I really began. Then I used to buy bundles of *El Sol* of Madrid and do my studying by looking these over. Little by little it all got away from me. For many years since then I have gone to Key West and stayed a few weeks every winter at the Casa Marina. Of course, this has not been possible these last two or three years, because that hotel has been in the hands of the Government and, since it is the only decent place there, I have not gone at all.

About Winters' *Anatomy:* Although I have a copy of the book I haven't read it and, in particular, have not read a line of his essay on my own poetry. This is out of pure virtue, because I think it disturbs one to read either praise or blame. There is something about poets, and probably about all writers, painters, musicians, etc., that makes them exceedingly eager for notice, which is a way of saying for praise. Moreover, they are easily and violently disturbed by the opposite; they will pay a degree of attention to hostile comment. Among other men not of their sort, as, for example, businessmen, politicians, etc., having to deal with the same sort of thing, it would not receive a moment's attention. But, since criticism is disturbing, whether it is favorable or unfavorable, I don't read it except occasionally, in the case of a man about whose judgement no question exists. I cannot say that that is true of Winters. Blackmur is immeasurably superior to him. I don't mean to say that he is any more intelligent, or any more sensitive, but he is more sensible, less eccentric. There is, however, a serious defect in Blackmur, or so it seems

1. This trip was later in 1923; Stevens meant to write five months instead of five years, or, possibly, his impressions may have been so different on his second visit with his wife that it seemed to be five years later (HS).

to me, and that is that it takes him twenty-five pages to say what would have been much better said in one. The result is that, after you have finished twenty-five pages of Blackmur, you haven't the faintest idea what he has been talking about. Either he has too many ideas or too few: it is hard to say which. How many ideas are there in currency that can be said to be purely Blackmurian ideas? Most critics very soon become identified with a group of principles or, say, a group of ideas; I cannot say that Blackmur is identified with anything. And the truth is that I don't know of any good solid books on modern poetry. Morton Dauwen Zabel[2] is a man of extraordinary intelligence, but it is hard to say to what he is primarily devoted. I think he is equally interested in both poetry and religion, and that creates a difficulty, because it inclines him to adopt some comparison with religion as the final test of poetry. However, I like Mr. Zabel more than these remarks might suggest.

The major men, about whom you ask, are neither exponents of humanism nor Nietzschean shadows. I confess that I don't want to limit myself as to my objective, so that in "Notes Toward A Supreme Fiction" and elsewhere I have at least trifled with the idea of some arbitrary object of belief: some artificial subject for poetry, a source of poetry. And major men are part of the entourage of that artificial object. All the interest that you feel in occasional frivolities I seem to experience in sounds, and many lines exist because I enjoy their clickety-clack in contrast with the more decorous pom-pom-pom that people expect.

Your mention of Alfonso Reyes is just the sort of allusion that makes me wish with all the excitement of a real wish that I knew Spanish better than I do. One grows tired of the familiar figures and to be able to find a fresh mind in a Mexican critic, or in the many writers in South America, and elsewhere in the Spanish-speaking countries, for which one would feel an instinctive respect would be a real excitement. It is, however, too late for me to attempt to become really familiar with another language.

I am sending you a copy of *Ideas of Order.* This I had not been intending to send until I could also send you a copy of *The Man*

---

2. Zabel (1901–64) was editor of *Poetry* magazine and author of *Literary Opinion in America* (New York: Harper, 1937).

with the Blue Guitar. As yet I have not been able to procure a copy
of *The Man With the Blue Guitar,* which will follow.

> Yours very truly,
> Wallace Stevens

> La Habana
> Feb. 13, 1945

My dear Mr. Wallace Stevens:

It was grand to hear from you again and to know that those
water-colors are cheering your rather gloomy house. I was surprised
to learn that your visit to Cuba was of twenty years ago, for your
poetry always has had for me a certain evocation of tropical light
and colors which I find quite charming and most unusual. Of
course, you know that Hemingway has lived among us for a long
time;[1] but I have always maintained that the milieu has not affected
him at all. I cannot see how anybody could not be impressed by certain *things* which I find completely absent in his most "Spanishied"
works. Of course, I have never quite come to admire Hemingway:
I mean that if you are a real blood and bone latino, you find absurd
and a bit of an affectation those "virile problems" which seem to
bother him so much. I sincerely think him an Illinois Puritan hunting for exotic sensations in the places and things which are naturally empty of all possibilities of adventure. I should not have said
PURITAN, because he is really more of a bourgeois and his dislike
of certain authors condemns him in my eyes. The fact that he has
had such a success makes me fear for that hierarchy of values which
must reign in a nation if its culture is not going to fall into the most
slappiest of arrangements. You are dead right, as you Americans
would put it, about Winters. Q: What about Mr. Yarmolinsky's
book about Modern Poetry?[2]

1. Since 1932, when he spent two months marlin fishing off its coasts,
Hemingway had called Cuba one of his homes. Near the end of the war
he gave his name and occupation to immigration officers as "E. Hemingway, Writer and Farmer," and settled into his *Finca Vigía* for a long stay.
2. With Babette Deutsch, Avrahm Yarmolinsky selected and translated
Modern Russian Poetry (London: John Lane, 1923) and *Contemporary
German Poetry* (New York: Harcourt, Brace and Company, 1923).

You will pardon my stupidity but I don't quite get what you mean by "major men." What do you mean by some "arbitrary object of belief"? I think it was more exact to call them a "source of poetry," but that too is rather ambiguous, eh? Is the intention mythological at all? Why do critics insist in calling you the Whistler of American poetry? What do you think of [John Malcolm] Brinnin's poetry and [Robert] Penn Warren?

I am very grateful for the promised volume of poetry. I will have all your poems here with me then. Are you ever returning to our lovely Habana?

> Yours modestly,
> José

About Hemingway—Picasso's "Guernica" and Dali's mystifying stories are Sp[anish] treatments of the same subject[,] not Romantic but macabre[,] in the tradition of Goya in the case of Guernica— Hemingway has not exploited the grotesque in our lives. Who has?

> [Hartford, Connecticut]
> February 26, 1945

Dear Mr. Rodríguez-Feo:

This is not a reply to your last letter, which I shall put off for a few days. But since I am sending two poems as part of a group to a magazine up here,[1] one of which bears your name, and both of which have a bearing on things that we have spoken of, I thought I had better send you copies.

The point of the poem that bears your name[2] is that, although the grotesque has taken possession of the sub-conscious, this is not because there is any particular relationship between the two things.

In the other poem[3] I have defined major men for you. I realize that the definition is evasive, but in dealing with fictive figures evasiveness at least supports the fiction. The long and short of it is that

---

1. "New Poems," *Voices* 21 (Spring 1945): 25–29. Poems included: "The Pure Good of Theory," "A Word with José Rodríguez-Feo," "Paisant Chronicle," "Flyer's Fall" (HS).
2. "A Word with José Rodríguez-Feo" (*CP*, 333–34).
3. "Paisant Chronicle" (*CP*, 334–35).

we have to fix abstract objectives and then to conceal the abstract figures in actual appearance. A hero won't do, but we like him much better when he doesn't look it and, of course, it is only when he doesn't look it that we can believe in him.

Very truly yours,
Wallace Stevens

[Hartford, Connecticut]
March 2, 1945

Dear Mr. Rodríguez-Feo:

I hope that my putting you in the position of deploring the act of the Moon in presiding over imbeciles was a permissible assumption.[1] After sending off my note with the poems, I came across the words *major men* in "Repetitions of a Young Captain."[2] In that poem the words major men merely mean the pick of young men, but major men as characters in humanism are different. Since humanism is not enough, it is necessary to piece out its characters fictively.

About Hemingway, I can say little because I don't read him. This is merely because I read little or no fiction, and really read very much less of everything than most people. It is more interesting to sit round and look out of the window.

I don't know Brinnin's poetry at all, and this is all wrong because he is doing a piece about me.[3] Of course, I know of him, but there has to be an enticement of reality in poetry. There is much more of that sort of thing in the work of Robert Penn Warren, or, if there is not more of it, there is more of my kind of reality. I share Warren's feelings in respect to the things that he feels about.

If you can find a copy of Thierry-Maulnier's *Introduction to French Poetry*,[4] published shortly before the war, by Gallimard, you

1. "As one of the secretaries of the moon,/The queen of ignorance, you have deplored/How she presides over imbeciles." "A Word with José Rodríguez-Feo" (*CP,* 333).
2. *CP,* 306–10.
3. "Plato, Phoebus and the Man from Hartford," *Voices* 21 (Spring 1945): 30–37 (HS).
4. *Introduction à la poésie française* (Paris: Gallimard, 1939).

will have as good an introduction to modern poetry as I know of. Specifically, it relates to French poetry, but it might just as well relate to all modern poetry.

A week or two ago, while I was in New York, I telephoned [Walter] Pach about Mariano.[5] He said that he did not know him; someone had spoken of arranging a meeting at a time when it was impossible for him. I spoke of you and he said that he had received a letter from you only that very morning. Since he spoke of you in the most friendly way, that makes you all right, because Walter is an old friend of mine. He is exceedingly full of admiration for everything Latin-American. This is particularly true in respect to Mexico, where he recently spent a long period of time. I spoke of Alfonso Reyes and, after listening to Walter, I couldn't wait to reach Hartford, where I immediately sent off an order for some of Sr. Reyes books.[6] True, I shall not be able to read them, but I shall get something out of them.

Very truly yours,
Wallace Stevens

5. Stevens had known and corresponded with Walter Pach (1883–1958) since his years in New York. Although Stevens criticized Pach's abstract illustrations accompanying the publication of "Earthy Anecdote" (in *The Modern School* 5, no. 7 [July 1918]: 193), he generally admired Pach's understanding of modern art and artists. José indeed corresponded with Pach on his own. When Pach's article "Problems of American Art" appeared in *Orígenes* in December 1944 (1, no. 4), Stevens discovered that he and José had this friend in common. Stevens' telephone call to Pach is confirmed in a letter Pach wrote José. Walter Pach to José Rodríguez Feo, 7 March 1945, in the possession of Rodríguez Feo. During the decade of the correspondence, Pach published books on Delacroix, Renoir, Miro, and Picasso; *The Art Museum in America* appeared in 1948 (Pantheon).

6. One of these books may have been Reyes' recently reissued *Juan Ruiz de Alarcon* (Cambridge: Harvard University Press, 1945), which was published separately after appearing as part of the Albert Schweitzer jubilee book edited by A. A. Roback; it had originally been published in 1917 (Madrid: Calleia). Little or nothing of Reyes' criticism or poetry had been translated into English by 1945, though it is possible that Stevens bought Reyes' poems in Spanish merely to have a glance through them, as he generally did with *Orígenes,* to use them in an intermittent effort to improve his Spanish. See José's suggestions in his letter of 23 March 1945.

[Havana]
March 5, 1945

My dear Mr. Stevens:

I am really overwhelmed by such diverse honors. But at the same time I cannot hide my crest-fallen feeling at the peek. For at first I thought the poems you sent were for *Orígenes*. I was partly confused by two facts 1) they were typed apart, 2) one of them bore my name. Naturally, I read them before taking notice of the infamous letter. That, later, told the sorrowful tale: they were intended for some American magazine. I was sorry because they both translate quite well; also I shan't veil my vanity at the hecho [the fact that]: a great poet finds it pleasant to converse with me. So I will close this very silly paragraph with the suggestion that perhaps the two poems could appear in the Spring number: our first anniversary number.

Your poems—*Ideas of Order*—came last week. I found your "Discourse" amazing. It has the essence of Habana; probably not as you found her last time you were here, but it partakes of what, without suspecting it, later would become its splenderous destiny. All brings to my mind the verse of [François de] Malherbe: "Et les fruits passeront les promesses des fleurs."

Did I tell you that *The Portrait of a Lady* appeared last month in Spanish[1] and hence I had to stop my trans. of the same? I am sending you *Les Impostures de la Poésie* de Roger Caillois. Perhaps, you shall have something to say about his brilliant chapter entitled "Pour Une Esthétique Sévère."[2] By the way, what do you think of Mr. [Robert] Lowell's poetry?[3] And Mr. [Randall] Jarrell's last poetry review in *Partisan?*[4]

1. *Retrato de una dama,* trans. Mariano de Alarcon (Buenos Aires: Emece Editions, 1944).
2. Paris: Gallimard, 1945.
3. Lowell's *Land of Unlikeness* had been published in 1944 by the Cummington Press, which that year also printed Stevens' *Esthétique du Mal;* the poems that would soon be collected in *Lord Weary's Castle* (1946) were appearing in quarterlies and journals.
4. Randall Jarrell, "Poetry in War and Peace," *Partisan Review* 12 (Winter 1945): 120–26. A review of books by Moore, Lowell, Williams, and H. D., and an anthology including Jean Garrigue, Eve Merriam, John Frederick Nims, Tennessee Williams, and Alejandro Carrión (HS).

I am sorry to close now but I have to go to the finca and want to send you this letter and the Caillois' book.

José Rodríguez-Feo

[Hartford, Connecticut]
March 19, 1945

Dear Mr. Rodríguez-Feo:

The Caillois book has just come, and I am happy to have it. Caillois is rather a sonorous *phraseur,* and this makes him a kind of intellectual Pierre Loti.[1] On the other hand, some people think that he is merely dry. The book that you have sent me was one that I had intended to order, so that your kindness in sending it is particularly pat.

About a poem for *Orígines* [sic]: I should rather do something specially for you than to have you use the two scraps that I sent you the other day. But it will take me some time to get round to this. I shall bear it in mind and perhaps, sometime during the coming summer, I shall be able to send you a poem.

You are probably a poet yourself, or so I gather. Only poets are really interested in poetry.[2] The time to read poetry is before you start to write it; after you start to write it you are afraid to read other people's poetry. Lowell's poetry is a case in point. Apparently, there is a considerable group of people who know his poetry; this may be because he is particularly keen from the Catholic point of view. But I have never studied any of his work because I don't want to pick up anything. In fact, there is probably no one who reads less poetry than I do. It takes very little to make people say that you nourish yourself on the work of other people and, since it is the easiest thing in the world to pick up something unintentionally, the safest plan is not to read other poets. Nor have I read Jarrell's review in *Partisan Review.* I remember seeing it.

1. Loti was a turn-of-the-century French dandy who wrote romance novels and cultivated public attention in his escapes involving travel, disguise, impersonation, and adventure.

2. José insists quite clearly, as he wrote recently, "I'm not a poet. I have written mostly literary criticism and that's all." Letter to Alan Filreis, 26 April 1983. He did write prose poems occasionally; one of these pieces, entitled "The Closed Door," was printed in *Orígenes.*

Finally, I spent a very pleasant half hour in Walter Pach's studio the other day. Washington Square has become a dreary old hole and, while Walter's studio gives it a touch of Paris, or perhaps Dresden, or, in view of the Indian carvings, a touch of Mexico City, it remains a dreary old hole, and as one's taxi starts uptown one feels a sense of satisfaction.

Yours very truly,
Wallace Stevens

[Havana]
March 23, [1945]

My dear Mr. Wallace Stevens:

The two poems you sent me a few weeks ago have been put into very elegant Spanish by Mr. [Eliseo] Diego and [Cintio] Vitier. I wanted to publish them in this Spring number, but fear it shall have to be postponed for the Summer. There are already two Americans in this issue—Brinnin and Levin—and there are already accusations of IMPERIALISM in the air.

I like what you said about reading. I am getting to prefer looking out of the window, also. Nevertheless, Chesterton has kept me from the window. I find him a most humorous, charming old fellow—e.g. "The Napoleon of Nutting Hill," "The Poet and the Lunatics," "The Father Brown's" yarns, and others. I have always disliked however his ultimate defense of the Catholic Faith; although it sustained for a longwhile his famous debates with Shaw and other sceptics. Today came a letter from Elizabeth Bishop, "la poetisa de Cayo Hueso," who has been very kind and offers an article on Valdés, a sort of Cuban primitive who lived most of his life in Key West.[1] I want to reproduce the article (which originally appeared in *Partisan*) with some fotographs of his work. Also, Mr. Pach wrote,[2] fully satisfied with the appearance of his little essay on American art in the Winter issue of *Orígenes*. Did you like it?

By the way, I hope you have received the Caillois book. At the

1. Bishop's essay about George Valdés appeared in *Orígenes* 2, no. 6 (July 1945): 27–32, with plates of Valdés' work photographed from the collection of Orson Welles.
2. On 7 March.

moment the review takes most of my time. This number is a sort of anniversary one and has more pages than the previous ones.

I haven't been able to obtain the book on Modern French Poetry which you recommend although I have seen other things by this Frenchman. I learnt yesterday that there is a gentleman in Habana who has it. Let's see if I can get in touch with him.

It is possible that I may go to the States this June. I have a sister in Philadelphia and will go to fetch her.[3] She will probably go to a camp in Vermont. Thus, I hope we shall have the opportunity to meet.

Yes, Brinnin admires you very much; and of course his poetry evidences the influence that your intentions have had on him. Of course, he does not share the luminosity of your later poetry; he is more at ease with "The Comedian as the Letter C." But there is more rhetoric than feeling in his work.[4] I think Reyes will bore you. He is a man whom you would love to meet and talk with. That is the brightness of Señor Reyes; but his poetry is only a competent combination of Spanish classical modes and Valery (with a little Mallarmé to cap it all). His best works are critical like the admirable "Criticism in the Athenian Age," "Cuestiones Estéticas," and his essay on Góngora, Mallarmé, etc.[5] But he is without doubt one of the most refined, cultured men in Latin America. Unfortunately he has dispersed his talents over many fields—a tragic fault in our best men, always. Reading now a most daring but charming book, *Les Dames Galantes* by Monsieur Brantôme.[6] This pornographic book tells the inside stories of the great princes and princesses of the age

3. Olga, after whom the family villa was named.

4. A case can be made for the influence of the early Stevens in, for example, *The Lincoln Lyrics* (Norfolk, Conn.: New Directions, 1942), a more ambitious series of poems than "Comedian," though later, in "Twelve or Thirteen Ways of Looking at Wallace Stevens," Brinnin would explicitly satirize Stevens' privileging rhetoric over feeling: "Not hissing esses, dank feathers in a pool—/But the idea of swans. . . ." *The Selected Poems of J. Malcolm Brinnin* (Boston: Little, Brown and Company, 1956), p. 93.

5. *La crítica en la edad ateniense* (Mexico: El Colegio de México, 1941); *Cuestiones estéticas* (Paris: P. Ollendorff, 1911); *Cuestiones gongorinas* (Madrid: Talleres Espasa-Calpe, 1927); *Mallarmé entre nosotros* (Buenos Aires: Editorial Destiempo, 1938).

6. Pierre de Bourdeille Brantôme (1540–1614).

of Francis the First and really puts to shame Mr. [Cyril] Connolly and Mr. [Henry] Miller's attempts.

I hope you will have interesting remarks sur Monsieur Caillois. By the way, Mariano will exhibit next November in N.Y. He is doing some beautiful things now. I wish you could come across the Channel and stay a while with us.

Yours sincerely,
José

How to translate "major men"? Vitier[7] simply calls them "les hombres grandes," but. . . .

7. Cintio Vitier (b. 1921), poet and prominent member of the Orígenes Group. His influential anthology, *Ten Cuban Poets, 1937–1947* (1948), included some of his own poetry. His *Fifty Years of Cuban Poetry, 1902–1952* (1952), assessed the importance of the *origenistas* and placed them in historical context. Volumes of his poetry include *Conjeturas* (1951), *Sustancia* (1952), and *Visperas, 1938–1953* (1953).

PUTTING TOGETHER A WORLD

1945–1947

Having been asked to respond to Roger Caillois, Stevens now had the opportunity to explain his literary tastes in a more systematic way. He also chose this moment in their four-month-old correspondence to explain how he felt about *Orígenes*.

Caillois' position was the awkward one of the rhapsodic rationalist. His small book, *Les Impostures de la poésie,* first appeared in Buenos Aires in 1944 in *Les Lettres Françaises,* a French-language journal with which Caillois had been associated since shortly after the fall of France. The thesis of this long essay was that the goal of the poet should be to describe a certain state of the soul. All in the name of clarity, Caillois offered a brutal and elementary assessment of modernist metaphysics, condemning any innovation that shattered versification. He approved of the poet Saint-John Perse, however, because he defended the order of culture against the idea of disorder in nature. With a few exceptions, one being Perse (also a favorite of José's), Caillois dismissed twentieth-century poets.

Apparently José believed that Caillois would appeal to Stevens' eclecticism. He did not consider the possibility that Stevens would probably not enjoy a polemical treatise by a man who would dismiss *him* as a mere metaphysical *phraseur.* José misread the tone of Stevens' criticism of the pamphlet, writing in response, "It was wonderful . . . to know you like Caillois!" It is wonderful, however, to read Stevens' response as he dismisses Caillois in exactly the lan-

guage others dismissed him: Caillois is a hyperrational man reject-
ing the unconscious as a source of poetry, yet presenting this very
position in a rush of lyricism. Stevens wrote to Henry Church: "The
curious thing about this is that [Caillois] pours himself out in a
perfect Niagara of poetic speech, so that, before you have read very
many pages, you feel that you are observing nothing more important than the struggle of one individual . . . against his own nature" (*L,* 495).[1]

It would take José until 1952 to find the occasion and courage to
say the same thing of Stevens. For now, however, José thought that
Caillois and his own literary review would strike a responsive chord.
As Stevens was drawn into the world of *Orígenes,* it became clear
to him why Caillois' odd detachment appealed to José. If Caillois
"dismisses and vulgarizes the idea of pure poetry," so in strikingly
similar terms (perhaps Caillois was a direct influence) José and his
fellow editors announced in the first number of *Orígenes* that "hap-
pily, those times are far away in which one talked of pure or imma-
nent art." Stevens' point in the spring of 1945, nearly a year after
the Allied invasion began to liberate Caillois' soil, was only this:
No clear-thinking man of letters would at that time propose *pure
poetry* without some world-weary qualification. Hence his dismissal
of Caillois as a man harping on an irrelevancy—it was hysterical at
worst, overstated at best. Similarly confused, Stevens ventured to
guess, were the pure poets of *Orígenes* who claimed to be reaching
out with "universalism" while obviously desiring most of all to look,
and remain, inward.

The Orígenes Group had now formed its own publishing house,
Ediciones Orígenes, and of the seventeen books of poetry they published between 1945 and 1954, twelve were by members of the

1. Stevens indeed would not have had to read many pages to come to
this conclusion. The opening sentence of Caillois' first chapter reveals the
personal bias Stevens criticizes: "I always feel more disposed to fight
poetry than to abandon myself to it" (p. 29). But there is reason to believe that Stevens felt similarly about abandoning himself to poetry and
that despite his immediate rejection, Stevens was significantly influenced
by Caillois' *sévère* approach to unconscious sources of verse. See Barbara
Farris Graves, "Stevens' Reading in Contemporary French Aesthetics:
Charles Mauron, Thierry Maulnier, Roger Caillois" (Ph.D. diss., University of Oklahoma, 1975), 117–57.

inner circle. The most important of these publications was Cintio Vitier's *Ten Cuban Poets, 1937–1947* (1948), which for the first time clearly identified the group's purposes, not by manifesto but by poetry: an antiregional, international modernism. Stevens saw a contradiction immediately in *Orígenes,* an assessment that became the basis of his later criticism of José. On the one hand José's group promoted "universalism," and on the other hand it was absolutely self-centered. José's talented young friends seemed untroubled by the fact that they referred to each other and their magazine so often that they were subject to accusations of elitism and hermeticism, criticism to which Stevens himself was especially sensitive. Even the fresh young Mariano painted oils *about* his friends and his aesthetic, such as one he entitled "Reading of Orígenes." Yet *this* painting led Lezama Lima to the remarkable conclusion that the group was never derivative and never "surrendered to flattery," that Mariano wished only, in Picasso's words, "To express what was within ourselves."[2]

José made a similar claim in writing to Stevens, testing the waters, as it were, between Havana and Hartford. He knew Stevens shared his anxieties about uses of art and he tried to convince Stevens that the *Orígenes* poets were writing for others and not themselves—for the world and not Cuba. Nationalism and not aestheticism was the root of decadence in modern art. Later, when *Ten Cuban Poets* was coming off the press, and obviously with the aim of his group in mind, José wrote: "I saw the Mexican show here. I finally came to the conclusion that Rivera, Orozco and Siqueiros are all terribly overrated and are really now embarked on an academic stage which reveal[s] their decadence. The Cubans are less pretentious, more charming and some have produced work which surpasses the bloody, screaming, cultural and nationalistic propaganda of the mejicanos."

After José sent Stevens a Mariano, the cubist rendering of a pineapple (which Stevens hung on the wall of his room and which became one of the sources of "Someone Puts a Pineapple Together"), Stevens naturally began looking in his copies of *Orígenes* for a mention of this young painter. He not only found Mariano and the

2. ". . . nada rendid al halago . . . sí de exprimir lo que había en nosotros." Lezama Lima, "Notes: Lozano and Mariano," *Orígenes* 1, no. 4 (December 1944): 44.

others mentioned there, but he found them in spades: *Orígenes* printed Angel Gaztelu's poem to Mariano; José and Lezama Lima both wrote essays about Mariano's painting; Lezama Lima's poem "Ronda sin Fanal—Para Mariano" describes one of Mariano's oils in heavily symbolic but obviously homosexual language. Stevens also saw Elíseo Diego's poem dedicated to Lezama Lima, Lezama Lima's to García Vega, Lorenzo García Vega's to Lezama Lima, and Lezama Lima's to Diego. The winter 1949 number would devote almost all of its pages to poems by *Orígenes* poets about each other or about the magazine itself. In a sequence of poems by Vitier, each of his friends became an abstraction—the canto to the sculptor Julian Orbon was called "Flechas," for his directness, his arrow-likeness; Fiña Garcia Marruz was "Automatic Reflexes" ("Reflexion del Instante"), perhaps for the seeming spontaneity of her line; Padre Gaztelu was a reverent "Hymn"; Elíseo Diego was, perhaps jokingly, "The Cloister" ("El Claustro"); and Lezama Lima, their best and purest poet, was "Arte Poética."

This hermeticism was easily and frequently attacked. To Stevens, who himself lived in and out of "his own matrix," the escapism of *Orígenes* was an aesthetic and personal but not a political problem. He was not angry but rather gently amused to find how seemingly detached from Cuba these Cubans were; he wrote to Henry Church: "My particular José dislikes the taste of Cuba; yet it is Cuba that has been his own matrix. His view is that of the platonic young intellectual. . . . He lives like the perpetual reader, without sex or politics" (*L*, 508). In a statement about his anthology, Vitier felt he had to defend *Orígenes:* "We are . . . very far from building that exquisite species of escapists that some imagine," he wrote, despising the "accusation of coldness, of obscurity and hermeticism [that] falls, more or less vaguely, over . . . the centrality of our poetic attitude."[3] Vitier, Lezama Lima, and José decided together on a line

3. "Estamos, pues, y a esto quería llegar, los poetas de mi reciente Antología, muy lejos de constituir esa exquisita especie de evadidos que algunos imaginan. Tan lejos, por lo menos, como lo estamos de ser los desarragaidos seguidores de las últimas escuelas europeas. Semejante asociación de equívocos no ha de parecer arbitraria si consideramos que una misma acusación de frialdad, de oscuridad y hermetismo recae, más o menos vagamente, sobre aquellas escuelas y sobre lo central de neustra actitud poetica." Vitier, "Ten Cuban Poets," *Orígenes* 5, no. 18 (Summer 1948): 41.

of defense: *Orígenes,* they declared, stood at once for "a poetry of exile and fidelity."[4]

Just as one should not have expected Stevens to see *his* Niagara of words in Caillois', so José and his friends should not have relied on his outright support of their effort to put together a world that transcended place. He finished Caillois just as he found María Rosa Lida's long article on Chaucer, which was so far from the regional or real that it was flatly academic. Although a year later he would write of *Orígenes* that "there is a surprising amount of elan to it," it was obviously time to tell José what he thought of the magazine.

[Hartford, Connecticut]
April 6, 1945

Dear Mr. Rodríguez-Feo:

I have now finished the Caillois pamphlet, after a good many interruptions. For one thing, it is an intelligent and sensitive discussion of something that is not discussed often enough and, moreover, of something that is of the greatest possible interest to me. All the same, I have seen, somewhere or other, a devastating review, and I myself feel very diffident about the thing. Even prose has eccentricities, and one of them is the inability of a good many writers of prose to do their job: that is to say, to write prose. That is the most striking characteristic of Caillois: he doesn't write prose; he writes poetry that looks like prose. When it comes to thinking a thing out and to stating it simply, he seems invariably to evade thinking by lapsing into a metaphor or parable and, in this way, he proves things, not by expressing reasons but by intimations to be derived from analogies. For instance, he concludes his pamphlet with a reference to Parmenides, whom he cites as a poet and apparently, from his point of view, as the supreme poet from the point of view of substance: a poet who develops a system of philosophy in verse.

I turned to Burnet's book[1] after reading this. I think that Burnet has said all there is to say in respect to the supremacy of a figure like Parmenides. Burnet says that he was the only Greek philoso-

4. "Una poesía del destierro y de la fidelidad." Ibid., 43.

1. John Burnet, *Early Greek Philosophy* (London: Adam and Charles Black, 1892) (HS).

pher to develop his system in verse. The sort of thing that he did was never able to maintain or perpetuate itself. Caillois is provocative, but he is also provoking; he is not a man with a first-class mind, nor even with a good mind. He says something that is untrue and then makes a great point of proving that it is untrue. This is a very easy thing to do; the good thinker says that something is true and then proves that it is true; this is not nearly so easy. Moreover, one constantly has the feeling that Caillois is influenced in respect to painting: for example, he dismisses and vulgarizes the idea of pure poetry: vulgarizes it by attenuating it and ridiculing it, using, for example the disappearing smile of the disappearing cat. But no one proposes to practice pure poetry. I think the feeling today very definitely is for an abundant poetry, concerned with everything and everybody.

There is something else that you have spoken of on which I should like to say a word or two, and that is the risk you run in respect to accusations of imperialism. I should say that the risk is not a risk in respect to imperialism but in respect to eclecticism. For instance, that article on Chaucer.[2] The act of editing a review is a creative act and, in general, the power of literature is that in describing the world it creates what it describes. Those things that are not described do not exist, so that in putting together a review like *Orígenes* you are really putting together a world. You are describing a world and by describing it you are creating it. Assuming that you have a passion for Cuba, you cannot have, or at least you cannot indulge in, a passion for Brinnin and Levin, and so on, at the same time. This is not a question of nationalism, but it is a question of expressing the genius of your country, disengaging it from the mere mass of things, and doing this by every poem, every essay, every short story which you publish—and every drawing by Mariano, or anyone else. The job of the editor of *Orígenes* is to disengage the identity of Cuba. I hope you won't mind my saying this. After all, I am not saying it for your sake, or for the sake of Cuba, but for my own sake. I agree with Caillois in this, at least, that there should

2. María Rosa Lida, whom Stevens criticizes for the article on Chaucer, studied medieval Spanish literature as much as English. She was editor of the selected works of the fourteenth-century poet Juan Ruiz (Buenos Aires: Editorial Losada, 1941).

be many things in the world: that Cuba should be full of Cuban things and not of essays on Chaucer.

A friend of mine[3] who usually lives in France writes:

> "I know Caillois very well, in fact he is one of my Poulains. We published his Mante Religieuse in one of the early numbers, his best I think. There is a certain secheresse about his thought *qui vous deroute.* You don't really know what to make out of him, whether he is an important writer, or a little phoney. Rimbaud was the god of his generation as he was of mine. Claudel is supposed to say a prayer to him every morning. But there is not much pure reason in Rimbaud, so what are you to make of it. Paulhan renie Rimbaud as does Michaux,—see the November *Horizon,* Toynbee article. Michaux told me the resembance is purely factice, coming from the common language, of the Ardennes.
> "But after all if there is the excitement in the struggle that is communicated by the book, *c'es deja quelque chose.* I have given up being exigent and am satisfied with little."

I am glad to hear that you are coming north sometime this summer. Do let me know when you are in New York and I shall be glad to come down and have lunch with you. I think that that would be the pleasantest arrangement because there is so little here in Hartford. I look forward to the pleasure of meeting you.

Very truly yours,
Wallace Stevens

[Havana]
May 5, 1945

My dear poeta:

It was wonderful to receive your letter and to know you like Caillois: you had so many interesting remarks to make! Today, I

---

3. Stevens' friend and correspondent since 1939, Henry Church, a patron of the avant-garde. Editor and co-founder of the French little magazine *Mesures,* he endowed the Mesures Lectures at Princeton; Stevens' "The Noble Rider and the Sounds of Words" (1941) was delivered during the first series of the lectures.

received a letter from the editor of *Circle,* a magazine published in Berkeley, and this young poet sends me a few of his poems for "my consideration." Do you know this gentleman, George Leite? Also, Henry Miller sends greetings from Big Sur and promises innumerable articles, short-stories and part of a novel! What a man! Hemingway has just returned; he is preparing a book of poems. Tells me he began as a poet. In the middle of the conversation, I asked him if he knew your work and he told me he thought you were a great poet. I think the ironic undertones of my question escaped him. Anyways, I am anxious to see those poems although it is beyond my poor calculating imagination to see old Hemingway writing poetry now. Eh?

Were you in N.Y. to hear the concert of Cuban chamber music played at the Museum of Modern Art? I hope that if you assisted you will have some remarks on this concert as we are all interested in hearing what you Americans think of our composers. By the way, I am listening as I write now to the second act of "Fidelio" played by Toscanini with the N.B.C. and singers of the Metropolitan Opera. It is one of those concerts they re-transmit for the troops overseas. It is really marvelous; specially since I have never listened to this opera before.

Now I am at work on an essay on *Moby Dick* since the Spanish translation has just appeared in South America.[1] I am taking the theme of isolation in the hero; here a Protestant hero with the significant meaning of loneliness as opposed to our *soledad.* Also, re-reading Proust, some of Gide (*Journal*). And James' *Varieties of Religious Experience* which I found most amusing since it contradicts that narrow view of pragmatism which still encumbers the real greatness of William James. He makes some truly amazing remarks on Platonism which made me think back on some of your poems: especially on the concept of the major men—if I may touch that theme once more. Have you ever read James' view on metaphysics?

I shall now leave you for it is late and they are playing the Overture Leonore and I am quite overcome. I think of you a great deal and the hope of seeing you soon makes me most glad and expectant. I have come to believe that a little gardening (I spend the morning

---

1. The translation was published in Buenos Aires by Emece Editores in 1944. José's article, "Moby Dick y El Aislamiento Heroico," appeared in *Orígenes* 2, no. 6 (July 1945): 15–21.

doing just that), a few books and the most resplendent memories and intuitions of what is to come some day to us again makes life beautiful. No need to expect more or ask for more.

> Your admirer Caribean,
> José

How grandiose the final chorus of *Fidelio* (Act II)! Very much like the end of the Ninth.

[Havana]
Junio 14, 1945

My dear Wallace Stevens:

I have not written sooner on account of the great amount of work which has piled up. The magazine is also on its way to the printer's. I really don't know why I suddenly thought of you, now. I am listening to Mr. Edwin Fisher playing Bach's Preludes and Fugues and reading Santayana's *The Middle Span* which has just arrived.[1] Wonderful afternoon indeed. Bach and Santayana and the pleasant memories and hopes! Do you suppose that if all men were as sensitive and shared the same things the world would be a finer, more pleasant place for us all? Or would we be bored by the monotony of elegance? Refinement, what is it then but a feeling of differentiation and a little, small sense of isolation? a selfish feeling or an egoist vision of our superiority to them, to the rest. Maybe it is also a sense of consolation, than an inferiority complex, a means of compensation (not in the silly Emersonian manner).

Also, re-reading *Le rouge et le noire.* I think however that *La Chartreuse* is immensely superior. Didn't he become a citizen of Milan?[2] Have you seen Jean Prevost's article on Stendhal—*La création chez Stendhal?* He has started a reaction against Flaubert and a movement to exonerate Stendhal. The essay came in the last issue of *Sur.*[3] I forget that you told me that the novel does not interest you at all. Well, what about actual poetry? What do you think of

1. *The Middle Span: Persons and Places* (New York: Scribner's, 1945), vol. 2.
2. Stendhal never became a citizen of Milan, though he spent much of his life there and considered it his home.
3. "La creación Stendhal a propósito de 'Rojo y Negro,'" *Sur* 125 (March 1945): 25–41.

the recent French works? Have you been able to purchase anything by [Henri] Michaux or [Louis] Aragon in New York? What has appeared in U.S.A. recently? Charles Henri Ford sent me his last book.[4] Pooh! The Tropical issue of *View* was the silliest, most unintelligent bit of Americana I have seen recently. Why perpetuate that stupid, tourist-exotic vision of our tropics?[5] M. Goll[6] does equally bad and Alexis Leger has not quite scaped the charm of romantic misinterpretation. Although I like him, we are translating his *Pluies*,[7] I questioned his sources and resources too.

What have you been doing lately? What about that poem you promised me for *Orígenes?* Remember?

I hope you are having a marvelous Spring. That's something I miss very much. Write soon. I am your devoted,

José Rodríguez-Feo

[Hartford, Connecticut]
June 20, 1945

Dear Mr. Rodríguez-Feo:

When I saw your letter this morning I thought it was going to tell me when you intended to be in this country, and I was disappointed. Even though there appears to be a vast difference between us in respect to our age, I am most interested in finding out how alike we are. For example, you are now interested in Stendhal. This is an intermittent interest; it comes back to you throughout life every few years. For me, Stendhal is the embodiment of the princi-

---

4. *A Night with Jupiter and Other Fantastic Stories* (New York: View Editions and Vanguard Press, 1945).

5. Series 5, no. 2 (May 1945), was a special issue edited by Paul Bowles. Picasso protégé Wilfredo Lam was the only Cuban featured in the issue.

6. Ivan (or Iwan) Goll (1891–1950). His *Lucifer Vicillissant* had appeared in 1944 (Paris: Editions R. A. Corrêa).

7. Alexis Saint-Léger Léger is Saint-John Perse (1889–1975). *Pluies* had appeared in French, with an accompanying English translation (*Rains*) by Denis Devlin, in the *Sewanee Review* 9 (1945). The "queerness" of St. John Perse's poems, Stevens wrote, "does not hurt them as poems" (*L*, 648). Perse later sent Stevens a copy of *Winds* (1953), which Stevens called "a pleasure" (*L*, 772).

ple of prose. I don't mean literary reality, but reason in its more
amiable aspects. No doubt Stendhal will survive Flaubert, because
Stendhal is a point of reference for the mature, while Flaubert is a
point of reference for the artist, and perhaps for the immature.
Flaubert takes possession of the immature and almost develops a
sense of maturity and of competence and strength. However, there
is an enormous amount of dust gathered about Stendhal. I have a
number of odds and ends of his that are not to be found everywhere,
but I have never made any attempt to collect any of the material
relating to him. This has been much overdone.

I like to hear you say "Pooh!" when you speak of Charles Henri
Ford. The young man who knows a little more about books, or a
little more about music than his neighbor is likely to be rather hard
to bear. But the young man who knows a little more about painting
than his neighbor is impossible. As a matter of fact, I don't think
that Ford knows much about anything; he is completely impossible.
All the same, he is clever and has created for himself a sphere in
which everything approves of him and is as he wants it to be. He is
having the best time in the world, and always has had, but he is as
untamed a snob as ever breathed, and *View* is a monument not to
silliness but to snobbery and in particular the snobbery of a young
man who knows a little more about painting than his neighbor, in
the sense that he knows an artist or two. God is gracious to some
very peculiar people. The hard part about all this is that I have
promised Ford a poem or two.[1]

The poem, or poems, that I shall send you will have to be written
during the summer, because I have been busy with something else
and, besides, I almost always dislike anything that I do that doesn't
fly in the window. Perhaps this has some bearing on what you call
"the monotony of elegance." To live in Cuba, to think a little in the
morning and afterward to work in the garden for an hour or two,
then to have lunch and to read all afternoon and then, with your
wife or someone else's wife, fill the house with fresh roses, to play
a little Berlioz (this is the current combination at home: Berlioz
and roses) might very well create all manner of doubts after a

1. "Analysis of a Theme" was published in *View* 5 (October 1945): 15
(HS).

week or two. But when you are a little older, and have your business or your job to look after, and when there is quite enough to worry about all the time, and when you don't have time to think and the weeds grow in the garden a good deal more savagely than you could ever have supposed, and you no longer read because it doesn't seem worth while, but you do at the end of the day play a record or two, that is something quite different. Reality is the great *fond,* and it is because it is that the purely literary amounts to so little. Moreover, in the world of actuality, in spite of all I have just said, one is always living a little out of it. There is a precious sentence in Henry James, for whom everyday life was not much more than the mere business of living, but, all the same, he separated himself from it. The sentence is . . .

"To live *in* the world of creation—to get into it and stay in it—to frequent it and haunt it—to *think* intensely and fruitfully—to woo combinations and inspirations into being by a depth and continuity of attention and meditation—this is the only thing."[2]

I am going to Cambridge next week to read a poem there at the exercises of Phi Beta Kappa, which are in a general way part of the Commencement activities.

I hope you received the copy of *Voices* that I sent you.

I am always happy to hear from you.

> Very sincerely yours,
> Wallace Stevens

[Havana]
July 1945

My dear Wallace Stevens:

Mil gracias for your delightful letter and the diverse, stimulating commentaries on Stendhal and Mr. "Pooh" Ford. How odd, that we

2. F. O. Matthiessen quotes this sentence from one of James' then unpublished notebooks in *Henry James: The Major Phase* (New York: Oxford University Press, 1944), 10; see Stevens' letter of July 1945. According to Matthiessen's edition of the notebooks, published a few years later, James' phrase was not "to think intensely" but "to think intently." Entry dated 23 October 1891, *The Notebooks of Henry James,* ed. F. O. Matthiessen and Kenneth B. Murdock (New York: Oxford University Press, 1947), 112. Matthiessen had been one of José's tutors at Harvard; Henry James was the subject of his senior thesis.

should always meet so serenely on all these views on art and life. Yes, we must be quite alike. I am 24 years old, you know? and yet I have always felt intellectually older, and emotionally like a baby. I signify, thus, the unavoidable inclinations: to children, flowers, toys, and laughter. And all these things tinged with a melancholy color. Let's not exult the roseate here! This morning a letter came from Mr. Lee ver Duft (lovely name) who is stationed in the Philippines and he sends a poem from his book—*Ho! Watchman of the Night, Ho!* (Gemor Press)[1] informs me that the book is to appear in Spanish and French translations and would like me to publish his poem in *Orígenes*. The poem—"Twilight"—appeared in *Circle,* vol. I, no. 4. Maybe you could consult that issue or his book and tell me what you think of his poetry. Might I add that you haven't told me your opinion of George Leite's poems[2]—he is the editor of *Circle.*

Your citation from James is delightfully personal. Is it from one of his letters? I am reading now Matthiessen's *Henry James.*[3] Speaking of books, I have just finished a wonderful, little travel (poetical) book: Henri Michaux's *Un Barbare en Asie.*[4] Also a dullish biography of Léon Bloy (who must have been a great bore himself) by dullish M. Colleye.[5] I do like some of Bloy's things, like *Letters to my Sweetheart.*[6] The rest of Cuba is reading atrocious books like *The Robe* and *The Keys of the Kingdom.* Amazing how mediocre taste will pervade when the nation who backs it up is powerful enough. The world will in time be inundated by vulgar, detestable American products, because America is all powerful and

1. Published in 1944 in a limited edition. In 1948 ver Duft's *The Double Heart and Other Poems* (New York: Panam, 1948) was published in a bilingual edition with Spanish translations by Feliz A. Ramirez, Pablo Mendez, and Roger Ferran.

2. George Leite had published *Ideas of Order in Experimental Poetry* (Berkeley: University of California Press, 1945). Its obvious debt to Stevens may have suggested to José an affinity between the younger and older poet. Leite edited *Circle: A Nova in the Arts* (1944–48) with Bernard H. Porter, and his poems had by then appeared in various quarterlies and reviews.

3. *Henry James: The Major Phase.*

4. Paris: Gallimard, 1933.

5. Hubert Colleye, *L'âme de Léon Bloy* (Paris: Desclée, 1930).

6. *Lettres à sa Fiancée* (Paris: Editions Stock, Delaman and Boutelleau).

can deliver the goods. Example: *The Readers' Digest* is the best
selling magazine in Latin America, *Red Amber* is a best seller to
the South, everybody says Thank you, O.K., never gracias, Muy
Bien, and the movies? Well, let's skip that one. . . . . .

I was very envious to learn of your visit to Harvard. I do miss old
Harvard very much.[7] I have just finished *The Middle Span* of Santayana, and I felt quite overcome by his reminiscences. By the way, do
you remember his essay on Proust's Essences? Where can it be
found?[8] Harry Levin spoke in a letter of his essay on Proust but did
not specify. Do you like Djuna Barnes's *Nightwood?*[9] I haven't read
it, but they say (so many people! For instance, Sweeney, JJ, who
certainly has taste and certain critical ability)[10] it is wonderful. I
would like to read and perhaps translate into Spanish. ¿Qué te
parece?

The climate here is very oppressive, hot and irritating. Is that
why Cuba's goddesses are Sex and Politics? Or is it because every-

7. We can be certain José wrote this letter prior to 19 July; on that day
Stevens summarized it for Henry Church: "My young man in Havana continues to send me letters of great interest. He abhors us to the extent that
we diffuse the *Reader's Digest* and *Forever Amber,* and similar vulgarities,
throughout Cuba and Latin America." Like his young Cuban friend, Stevens seemed to "miss old Harvard very much": "The truth is that these
occasional returns to Cambridge seem to get at something one vitally needs
and that this is all the more true when one meets people there. I suppose
most of one's gusto (the sort of thing that bothers the Cuban) is the result
of isolation" (*L,* 508).

8. "Proust on Essences" was published originally in *Life and Letters* 2
(1929): 455–59. It was more easily available to José in *Obiter Scripta*
(New York: Scribner's; London: Constable, 1936), 273–79, or in *The
Triton Edition of the Collected Works of George Santayana* (New York:
Scribner's, 1937), 14:175–79.

9. With an introduction by T. S. Eliot (New York: Harcourt, Brace
and Co., 1937).

10. James Johnson Sweeney, art critic, became director of the Guggen-
heim Museum in 1952. Sweeney frequented Barbara Church's Park Avenue
gatherings, where Stevens saw him. José undoubtedly knew of Sweeney's
many books on contemporary art; during the period of the correspondence,
Sweeney authored or edited books on Stuart Davis (1945), Alexander
Calder (1946), Marc Chagall (1946), Henry Moore (1947), Mondrian
(1948), Hans Hartung (1950), Jean Miro (1953), and African folktales
and sculpture (1952).

body *knows* and are bored to death, before actually dying, of everything. The terrible gap with us is intelligence! And really there
cannot be passion without intelligence, or courage or real hatred—
Platonic, yes, but then all goes back to good old Plato who I realize
must be your favorite boy too!

I shan't be able to go to the States until December if at all. But
then why don't you come down for a vacaciones. There is so much
more to see here and the view is always stimulating! Write soon
and tell me of Leite and the Dutchman's poetries.

Carinosamente,

José

P.S. Do you [know] Matthiessen or Harry Levin—very intelligent
and stimulating men. The best at Harvard. I think so, modestly. I
hope you won't mind (I am enclosing a picture of myself) the picture, just so you have an idea of what your correspondent looks
like.

[The first page of Stevens' reply is missing.]

[Hartford, Connecticut]

[July 1945]

This is merely something that I have heard. Such letters as I have
had from her have been everything that you would expect from a
woman of extraordinary humanity and extraordinary delicacy.[1] At
the present time she seems to be cooperating a good deal with Jan
Hugo, an artist, particularly in prints of different types. Before the
war, Hugo was beginning to make a great stir in Paris; New York
is definitely not the place for him. I sent Gemor Press a check the

---

1. Stevens is referring to Anaïs Nin. In 1944 he had encouraged a friend
to contact her in New York about her handpress publications. He jokingly
noted that "she could probably produce interesting capital letters and all
that," yet was obviously impressed with "the highly sensitive sort of thing
that she does." Wallace Stevens to Hi Simons, 6 September 1944, Huntington Library. Since 1920 Nin had been married to printer, designer, and experimental filmmaker Ian Hugo. Her *Under a Glass Bell* appeared in February 1944 with seventeen of Hugo's engravings printed in relief from
copper plates. In 1945 Gemor Press issued Nin's *This Hunger* with five
colored wood-block prints by Hugo.

other day for something and it seems to have been cashed at the Sevilla Bar in New York. Probably it helped everybody to get through a rainy afternoon.

Djuna Barnes I am not able to take seriously. But I think you are wrong about Léon Bloy. Some years ago I collected Bloy and he made a great impression on me, but I have no idea what became of his books, and what I should think of him in the atmosphere of today I don't know. The mere atmosphere has vitiated a lot of things.

Finally, about Matthiessen: the quotation from Henry James about dwelling in the world of creation will be found on page 10 of Matthiessen's *Major Phase*. That is all I know about it. I have met Matthiessen, but am not familiar enough with his work to have any ideas about him. Harry Levin I know only from odds and ends.

Very sincerely yours,
Wallace Stevens

P.S. I am glad to have the picture of you. Alas, I have nothing that I can send in return. Then too, I have forgotten to comment on your remark that knowledge is an exacerbation of futility: it all depends. In the case of pure Platonism, which is, I suppose, the typical disease of young men of 24 or 25, yes. But we used to have here in Hartford a "preacher," Horace Bushnell, in whose memory his family has erected a hall costing some millions of dollars.[2] On an entablature on the facade there is inscribed the following quotation, which I am obliged to quote from memory:

> Life is insipid to those who do not have great works in hand and who are without lofty aims to elevate the feeling.

Conceding the pomp in this, nevertheless it is an intensely true thing, and people who yield to such an idea are not the sort of people that die of Platonism.

W.S.

2. Bushnell Memorial Hall, where Stevens and his wife sometimes attended concerts.

[Havana]
August 31, 1945

My dear Wallace Stevens:

Your poems[1] arrived successfully, full of that lucidity and nobility which your last style revealed. I have given them to a Cuban poet whom I trust more than myself since his poetic insight will suffice and probably render the poems with more exactitude than my insufficient manipulation of the language. I hope to publish them in the next issue or if the pagination is too exuberant in the Winter number.

I am quite busy now, writing an essay on Scott Fitzgerald for *Sur*.[2] I have here his last volume, edited by Mr. Wilson—*The Crack-Up*.[3] Also, in the intervals I read a story of Magic by M. Levi,[4] the queer gentleman who was such an influence on Villiers and Rimbaud. Also, speaking of Rimbaud, I am reading his letters[5] and a biography, really delicious, of M. Poquelin by Ramon Fernandez. His observations on *Les précieuses ridicules* are really illuminating. I suppose you know this great French critic and have read his things.[6]

Now the British Council wants to give me a scholarship to go and study a year at Cambridge University. I have been recom-

1. *Orígenes* 2, no. 8 (Winter 1945): 3–6. "Cuatro Poemas" by Stevens, translated by Oscar Rodríguez Felíu, contained: "Unidad de las imagenes" ("Thinking of a Relation between the Images of Metaphors," *CP*, 356–57), "El caos movil e inmovil" ("Chaos in Motion and Not in Motion," *CP*, 357–58), "La casa y el mundo en calma . . ." ("The House Was Quiet and the World Was Calm," *CP*, 358–59), and "Conversación con un hombre silencioso" ("Continual Conversation with a Silent Man," *CP*, 359–60) (HS).

2. It was never published.

3. New York: New Directions, 1945.

4. Sylvain Lévi (1863–1935), whose interests were Buddhism, Indian literature, and Sanskrit.

5. *Lettres de la view littéraire d'Arthur Rimbaud* (Paris: Gallimard, Éditions de la Nouvelle revue française, 1931).

6. Ramon Fernandéz (1899–1944), the "pale Ramon" of Stevens' "Ideas of Order at Key West," wrote a biography of Jean Baptiste Poquelin (Molière) entitled *La vie de Molière* (Paris: Gallimard, 1929). We may assume that Stevens did not know Fernandéz' work despite his use of the name: "Ramon Fernandéz was not intended to be anyone at all. . . . as I might have expected, [it] turned out to be an actual name" (*L*, 798).

mended by Prof. Blackstone of Cambridge Univ., who recently delivered a series of lectures on modern English literature. He is writing a very good book on Blake, which the Cambridge University
Press will publish shortly.[7] But I don't know what to do. Leaving
Cuba now will be a great derision to many. I have so many things
to do here and, at the same time, I would love to spend a year in
England. What do you think?

Anaïs Nin sent her book of stories—*Under the Glass Bell*.[8] I have
translated one of her stories for *Orígenes*. I learned that all restric-
tions for Americans are erased. You can travel to Cuba now without
a passport. Won't you consider a trip to Habana in your next vaca-
tions? It would be so wonderful, for us, if you came down. I read
part of your Phi Beta Kappa poem in the Harvard Bulletin and like
it very much.[9] Are you preparing the publication of a new book of
poetry? Have you seen Levin's essay on Stendhal?[10] Have you read
Maurice Scève, the French poet, whom I find so many times ab-
sconded in the poetry of Paul Valery?[11]

Habana is very hot now. I expect to go to Varadero, the wonderful beach near Cardenas next week and try to finish there my essay
on Fitzgerald. Then I shall write again, impregnated with a little
more salt (the pun on *sal* which in Spanish means humour). At
the moment, I am a little tired and depressed and that is no mood
to converse with our friends.

Again, thanks for the lovely present.

Yours ever,
José

7. Professor Bernard Blackstone (b. 1911), whose *English Blake* was
published by Cambridge University Press in 1949, also wrote *Virginia
Woolf: A Commentary* for the Hogarth Press (1949).

8. First published as *Under a Glass Bell and Other Stories* (New York:
Gemor Press, 1944).

9. "Description Without Place" (*CP*, 339–46) was read at the Phi Beta
Kappa exercises at Harvard in June 1945; it was published in the *Sewanee
Review* 53, no. 4 (Autumn 1945): 559–65. See Stevens' letter of 20 June
1945.

10. *Toward Stendhal* (Murray, Utah: Modern Library, 1945).

11. Maurice Scève was a sixteenth-century French poet.

Oct. 9, 1945
At Villa Olga

My dear Wallace Stevens:

I beg your pardon for this long silence. You do not know how much our conversations have come to mean to your savage Caribbean. But my mother has become sick again and I have had to interne her in a sanitorium. To see the process of disintegration of her mind has been a great sorrow to me although she has been getting ill that way since she was eighteen; but one never gets used to it. Now I expect she will be there for three or four months for the crisis this time has been less grave than before. That has kept me quiet and melancholic for a long time, but I feel better now. Tomorrow I am taking to press the autumn issue of *Orígenes*.

Your poems will appear in the Winter issue. They have been translated by our friend, Rodríguez Felíu. What are you doing now? Have you published any more poems recently? Are you planning any new book of verse? I have been re-reading Rilke's *Elegies of Duino* which I like very much.[1] The *Sonnets to Orpheus*[2] are next in line. Also, I just finished a wonderful book, *Ideas for a biological conception of the world* by the Baron Jakob von Uexkull.[3] There this great biologist comes to the conclusion that life's origin cannot be explained by material motives, refuting Darwin, and that Plato was nearer to the truth when he imagined the archetypes as the sources of all our ideas and beings. Curious, eh? Also, read Claudel's *L'Annonce faite à Marie,*[4] and Péguy's *Notre Jeunesse.*[5] Péguy's book is a remarkable commentary on our actual situation. I won't be surprised if De Gaulle keeps this juicy volume at his bedside. He should.

I am living now at my little country place, Villa Olga, near Habana. I am alone there and have only the company of the Negro

1. *Duino Elegies,* bilingual edition in German and English, ed. J. B. Leischman and Stephen Spender (New York: Norton, 1939).

2. Bilingual edition in German and English, trans. M. D. Hertor Norton (New York: Norton, 1942).

3. *Bausteine zu einer biologischen Weltanschauung: Gesammelte Aufsätze* (Munich: Fr. Bruckman, 1913).

4. *L'Annonce Faite à Marie, mystère en quatre actes et un prologue* (Paris: Gallimard, 1927).

5. Paris: Cahiers de la quinzaine, 1910.

cook who never says a word. I am writing and reading a great deal. I tend my garden and feed the chickens and the Negro takes care of my lovely black and white cow, Lucera, and the mule, Pompilio. I came into town last night to hear Brailowsky give a marvelous recital of Chopin.[6] It is prodigious, his playing of Chopin. It was a revelation to hear his interpretation of the Polish master. Did you see that horrible film, *A Song to Remember?*[7] Did you look Scève up? I think I misspelled his name in my last reference to you. I read Valery's essay on Stendhal too.[8] Have you read J. Rivière's *Rimbaud.*[9] I found it rather silly; his explanation of Rimbaud via calling him an innocent angel lost in this bad, confused world where he was not destined to prosper is rather childish. There are passages however of great interest. But why write such nonsense? From now on, I abhor all exegesis of poems. Rimbaud's letters are really amazing, especially the one where he puts down his idea of the poet as a seer who must become a medium through a long and reasonable effort and thus disintegrate his *senses* until he arrives at the Unknown. Speaking of the angelic character of Rimbaud, I remember now Valery's witty remark: "What would the men of intelligence and wit do with themselves if there were no original sin?" But then that life is necessary, for all we live through and come to know and suffer remains as the possible fountain of wisdom or love for others. That is why I believe we should never reject even the great lies of history. They too can be useful to weave the pattern of obscurity. A case here to illustrate: Rilke. So much effort to hide things and he comes to succeed only in *making* that effort. When he really obscures things, his poems failed. That is why one feels so many dull moments in reading him. I cannot but think that he repeated himself too much. His paradox can be summed up in these simple words of Proust: "On ne peut être fidèle qu'a ce dont on se souviant, on

6. The Russian-born pianist (1896–1976) presented the complete works of Chopin in a cycle of six recitals on Chopin's own piano.

7. Starring Paul Muni and Merle Oberon, the film was directed by Charles Vidor (1945).

8. *Essai sur Stendhal* (Paris: Éditions de la Pleiade, 1927). José was more likely to find it in *Variété deuxième volume* (Paris: Éditions de la N.R.F., 1937), where it was reprinted along with nine other Valéry essays from the 1920s.

9. Jacques Rivière, *Rimbaud* (Paris: Editions Kra, 1930).

ne peut se souvenir que de es qu'on a connu" (in a letter to Madame Scheikévitch).[10]

I hope if things do not get worse here to be in New York by Xmas. I am going to stay with my little sister, Olga, in N.Y. I hope to see you then. By the way Mariano, the painter, is in New York now. He will exhibit in the Feigl Gallery in November; address Feigl Gallery Madison 601 at 57th. I am sure he would like to see you there; if you can make it. Have you seen Margarite Young's *Angel in the Forest?*[11] I find it quite entertaining.

I must close now for the groceries have arrived and the man talks endlessly. Otherwise there will be no end to this letter. There is no end however to the pleasure that I receive in reading your marvelous messages from Hartford and you know that my admiration and affection grow in *ausencia* each day.

My best and most cordial saluations,
Pepe

[Hartford, Connecticut]
Oct. 17, 1945

Dear Caribbean:

I have not been able to write to you, partly because of the illness of my stenographer, but the news of Pompilio calls for particular attention. In fact I have spent a little time thinking about life in the Villa Olga: the young man of letters confronting the Negro, not to speak of Lucera, the embodiment of the male principle. Possibly the Negro and Pompilio are interchangeable. The truth is that I have been thinking a bit about the position of the ignorant man in what, for convenience, may be called society and thinking about it from this point of view: that we have made too much of everything in the world and that perhaps the only really happy man, or the only man with any wide range of possible happiness, is the ignorant

10. "One can only be faithful to what one remembers, one can only remember what one has known." Letter to Marie Scheikévitch, November or December 1915, in *Letters of Marcel Proust,* ed. Mira Curtiss (New York: Random House, 1949), 287.

11. *Angel in the Forest: A Fairy Tale of Two Utopias* (New York: Reynal & Hitchcock, 1945).

man. The elaboration of the most commonplace ideas as, for example, the idea of God, has been terribly destructive of such ideas. But the ignorant man has no ideas. His trouble is that he still feels. Pompilio does not even feel. Pompilio is the blank realist who sees only what there is to see without feeling, without imagination, but with large eyes that require no spectacles.

Your group at the Villa Olga absorbs me. Of yourself you say that you read and write and cultivate your garden. You like to write to people far away about such unreal things as books. It is a common case. I have a man in Ceylon with whom I have been exchanging letters for some years.[1] He is an Englishman, an Oxford man and a lawyer, I believe, but actually he makes his living and the living of his family by growing coconuts at a place called Lunawila in the province, or parish, or whatever it may be called, of Kirimetyana. In the depths of his distance from everything he extracts, because he needs to extract, from poetry and from his reading generally far more than you and I extract from the things that we have in such plenty, or that we could have because they exist in such plenty near at hand.

Somehow I do not care much about Lucera. I imagine her standing in the bushes at night watching your lamp a little way off and wondering what in the world you are doing. If it was she, she would be eating. No doubt she wonders whether you are eating words. But I take the greatest pride in now knowing Pompilio, who does not have to divest himself of anything to see things as they are. Do please give him a bunch of carrots with my regards. This is much more serious than you are likely to think from the first reading of this letter. We have here a bootblack, that is to say, a man who comes here several times a week. Very often he talks about himself and his early life. He was a shepherd in Italy when he was a boy. He uses figures of speech like this: I was tired and laid down under a tree like a dog. In this there is no exaggeration. It is hardly even a figure of speech. It is pretty much the same thing as you, yourself, seated under a tree at the Villa Olga and realizing that the world is as Pompilio sees it, except for you, or that the world is as the Negro sees it because he probably sees it exactly as Pompilio sees it. But

1. Leonard C. van Geyzel.

Lucera sees it in a special way, with the gentleness and tenderness visible in her look.

This has left me very little space to speak of things that you have been reading. I think, therefore, that I shan't speak of them at all, but instead try to raise a question in your mind as to the value of reading. True, the desire to read is an insatiable desire and you must read. Nevertheless, you must also think. Intellectual isolation loses value in an existence of books. I think I sent you some time ago a quotation from Henry James about living in a world of creation. A world of creation is one of the areas, and only one, of the world of thought and there is no passion like the passion of thinking which grows stronger as one grows older, even though one never thinks anything of particular interest to anyone else. Spend an hour or two a day even if in the beginning you are staggered by the confusion and aimlessness of your thoughts.

Last night I took Mariano's second water color out of the case in which I keep such things and put it in a frame. This is the drawing of a woman seated in a fauteuil and yet in her bare feet. There is a curious, easily-recognizable Cuban coloring and manner in this. I have not hung it before, unlike the sketch of the pineapples which I hung at once, because I wanted to have a special frame made for it, yet I have been so infrequently in New York that I thought I might as well put it together myself, as I did. I shall try to see Mariano's exhibition.

There is a note on Scott Fitzgerald in this month's *Partisan* by Mr. [Andrews] Wanning.[2] It is very well done. It is curious that Fitzgerald should have been interested in so many people merely because they had money and lived in luxury. The richest man I know seems not to be conscious of the fact that he has any money at all and luxury is repulsive to him.[3] However, he went to Europe as a boy to study music and has lived in France ever since and in France, if anywhere, one's attitude towards money and luxury, while it exists, is ameliorated by so many other things that do not exactly crowd us here.

You won't forget to take a look at Pompilio from my point of

2. "Fitzgerald and His Brethren," *Partisan Review* 12 (Fall 1945): 545–51 (HS).
3. Henry Church.

view. Don't paint any pictures of the hereafter for him. Don't tell him about the wonderful weather in your Eastern provinces. Give him a bunch of carrots and swear at him in a decent way, just to show your interest in reality.

Always yrs,
Wallace Stevens

[Havana]
Oct. 20, 1945

My very dear friend:

How opportune the arrival of your charming letter! I had just taken a wonderful bath (it is 12:40 morning, bright skies of azure tinges and a subtle breeze that spells perhaps a great hurricane or then a nice afternoon at the ball game. Yes, I go to such things: today the Almendares plays again the Habana[1] in the inaugural game. Oh, it is silly but I find the people who go to this affair, a baseball game, amusing and really more interesting to talk to than most of the so-called clever fellows, of course I do not speak of really intelligent people like Lezama or Mariano) and this bath was the first bath after four days with an acute attack of sinusitis which makes me very miserable. For that reason I have deserted Villa Olga. I had no one to take care of poor Pepe there. Pompilio is very indifferent in these matters and Lucera, well, she just makes funny faces and goes on chewing her pensive leaves of grass. I was delighted to read the little discourse on my animals (they are not worthy of such elegant attention) and most assured by your opinion on the ignorant man. I say "assured" because I have many such ignorant men for friends and I have been criticized bitterly by some of my literary friends who consider *it* a waste of time and a contamination. "Think of your Spanish and your *modales* (manners)" they exclaim. Sometimes they accuse me of having the democratic virus and cite Baudelaire to reinforce their silly ideas. Of course, all these lads are the very ones who are so bored most of the time, and come to Villa Olga to entertain themselves, or their souls. They are amazed at the fact that I am contented, occupied and even a little

1. The teams were rivals.

fatter. They all go away, however, for the city has too many shallow distractions for such people.

I agree with you, old wise man (how old are you anyway? I hope the old won't disgust you) in that I do not think as much as I should. But remember that thinking is a difficult process and I did much rather look at Pompilio eating his oats or just converse with Evaristo, a blond *güajiro* who comes to bring the groceries. I will try to think more intensely and precisely as you recommend.

I saw an article, very poor indeed, on your genre of *poesía* in the latest *Sewanee*.[2] I could not define your poetry so easily, but I like it very much and read it quite often. In that *Sewanee* came the Phi Beta Kappa poem which I had already read (fragments) in the *Harvard Bulletin*. Of lately I have been reading only poetry, 16 and 17th century Spanish poetry which is marvelous. That is enough for a few months, with our daily exercises of gymnastic thought.

My essay on Scott Fitzgerald is gathering moths in the deepness of a drawer.[3] I came to him with the best of intentions but he bores me so and there are so many more interesting things to read and do. . . . I am coming to regard reading now as a close circle and only the most excellent of poets and writers get around the circle. For instance, I discover that I knew nothing of the French theatre: Racine, Molière and Corneille were unknown figures although I had gone thru the gestures of perusing some of their plays when learning French. I must therefore spend some time in their wonderful world, above all Molière's.

I might close by reiterating my invitation to have you lock up the Insurance and take a trip to Habana this winter. If you decide to do that, let me know in time. Otherwise, I might go to N.Y. this Xmas to see my sister Olga.

An affectionate embrace,
José

Did I ever talk to you of *Linda,* my lovely (she) dog—how do you say *perra?*

2. Hi Simons, "The Genre of Wallace Stevens," *Sewanee Review* 53, no. 4 (Autumn 1945): 566–79.

3. See José's letter of 31 August 1945.

[José wrote the following note on a card announcing a new exhibit of Mariano.]

[Havana]
[October–November 1945?]

Dear Mr. Stevens:

I hope you can find a moment to see Mariano's new paintings. He wishes to know your reactions to his latest things.

Pepe

or

José

[Hartford, Connecticut]
November 26, 1945

Dear Mr. Rodríguez-Feo:

I ought long since to have sent a word to you about Mariano's exhibition,[1] but I was a bit baffled by its incendiary characteristics. When it comes to speaking of pictures that I don't quite understand, discretion requires thinking about them. Of course, I am not able to talk about the pictures except in the most general way. Having formed my impressions of Mariano from the two water colors that you sent me and which are now hanging in my room at home, I was a bit set back by the unexpected force of color and violence of color in the paintings. There was a note to the effect that Mariano had studied in Mexico. There was nothing to show that he had studied in Europe. I don't know what the facts are. However it may be with other people, the painting of the Mexicans, even the most notable of them, has always seemed to me something of a folk art.[2] This is

1. "Mariano: Oil Paintings, Gauches, Drawings," Feigl Gallery, 17 October–3 November 1945. Stevens saw twenty-seven pieces by Mariano, including "Church on the Outskirts of Habana," "Cuban Farmers," "Cockfight," "Bathers," and "Reclining Woman with Cat."
2. The Orígenes Group did understand Mariano's art as essentially violent, noting, in Lezama Lima's words, his "excessive exigencies" ("excesivas exigencias") and "the wave of movement directed to frenzy" ("la onda de movimiento dirigido al frenesí"). "Notes: Lozano and Mariano,"

true notwithstanding that many of the most remarkable of the
Mexican painters have studied in Europe, and, by Europe, I don't
mean only Paris. But if I did mean only Paris, it would be important because in my own case that French school seems to be the
international medium. Then another thing about Mariano: it often
happens in the case of an artist big enough to include a number of
extremes that his basic character is one of those extremes and not
a composite of all of them. In other words, one of the extremes is
natural and the others are somehow not true. For instance, in the
case of the music of Sibelius one cannot help feeling that his identity is really to be found in melancholy melody. Sibelius, himself,
recognizing this, forces himself, with the concealment typical of so
many of us, to the opposite extreme and writes score after score of
the harshest and most discordant, most vigorous music. But the
source of all this is the melancholy melody. In the same way, it is
commonplace for excessively imaginative writers to try to escape
from their imagination in realism and in no end of realistic detail,
as, for example, Kafka. To take a case a little nearer at hand:
Hemingway. No-one can read more than a few pages of Hemingway without becoming very much aware of the fact that he is a poet.
Consequently, I was not at all surprised when you said in your recent letter that he was thinking of publishing a volume of poems.
While it may be quite extraordinary in form and expression, still I
haven't the slightest doubt that what Hemingway will be trying to
get at is what everyone instantly recognizes to be poetry. So with

---

Orígenes 1, no. 4 (December 1944): 44. But the *origenistas* would
have been appalled at Stevens' notion that Mariano might be masking his
true self in easy folkloric expression. As both a publication and a literary
movement *Orígenes* claimed to have nourished a truly Cuban sensibility,
"which redeems [the movement] from the abominable folkloric . . . seen
up to now as the only solution to confirm that which is ours" ("que nos
redime del abominable realismo folklórico y costumbrista visto hasta ahora
como única solución para fijar lo nuestro"). Quoted from the words of
Alejo Carpentier by Lezama Lima in "Signs," 9, no. 31 (1952): 66. Certainly José and his friends agreed that Mariano had been influenced by
Mexican art, but as to the painter's folklore, it was "an *ironic* interpretation of our 'national reality' " ("en esta irónica interpretación de nuestra
'realidad nacional' "). José Rodríguez Feo, "The Works of Mariano and
His New Aesthetic," 1, no. 3 (October 1944): 43; editors' emphasis added.

Mariano, I don't know enough about him to improvise as to his true identity, but my guess is that it is not to be found in these torrential paintings. I am sorry to have missed seeing him. He was not in the Gallery when I was there. Apparently his exhibition was successful because a good many of the pictures seemed to have been sold. Such strong paintings usually require a readjustment of everything near them at home. However, it is clear that Mariano is a man of great vitality and that in the long career that lies ahead of him he will accomplish much.

I notice that Portocarrero and Mario Carreño are having shows in New York. Carreño has even achieved the Knoedler Galleries. Portocarrero's things seemed to have met with a bit of diffidence. I was not able to see them. I have not seen any comment on Carreño's show. In fact, there is very little comment on paintings in the New York papers nowadays and what there is is a waste of time.

I look forward to the possibility of your making a visit to New York during the holidays and, if you really do and will let me know, I shall be happy to come down and have lunch or some such thing with you. There is not the slightest chance of my going to Cuba or anywhere elsewhere for the present. I should like to take a trip through the air and go several thousand miles straight up and there explode into no end of stars, which from a distance would read, in Spanish, "regards to Pompilio."

Very sincerely yours,
Wallace Stevens

[Havana]
February 15 [1946]

My dear Wallace Stevens:

Due to my long sickness I have not sustained the dialogue, but I thought and wondered about you. Your marvelous poems are appearing in the Winter issue,[1] I am sending copies apart, and we regret it has delayed its coming-out but the finances of *Orígenes* are so shaky that we don't know ever for certain when the thing

---

1. The winter 1946 issue (vol. 3, no. 12, pp. 12–13) contained José's translation, "Tentativa por descubrir la vida," with the English on a facing page.

will be possible. I want to thank you again for your collaboration, kindness and beautiful patience in putting up with us and giving our magazine the privilege of printing America's first poetry. The translations are probably the best you can get; far superior to those made for *Sur* by Borges and Bioy—and that is saying a great deal![2] I myself was astonished when Rodríguez Felíu handed them in for your poetry is quite difficult to apprehend and its flavour can escape easily a less conscious and artistic effort.

I am planning a trip to Oriente, the western province of Cuba, to rest. There I expect to finish my essay "The Masks of Henri Beyle." By the way, I quote there the sagacious remarks you made about Stendhal in a letter you wrote me a while ago. I hope you don't mind. What are you doing now? Have you published any new poems? Tell me: what new American poets do you like best? Have you seen Byron Vazakas' things?[3]

I have taken to smoking cigars ever since Churchill landed in Habana with a big smile and a cloud of smoke. I felt sort of humiliated by the whole thing and promised myself never to go around gaping at the great men. Of course, I only admire him because he wrote a solid history of the Duke[4] and once expressed a frantic admiration for T. E. Lawrence. Did you ever come across Blackmur's essay on the Colonel Lawrence—in "The Expense of Greatness." It's the best appreciation I have read of his non-*fiction* and style.[5]

Mariano has just given me a beautiful portrait of Paul Valery, a

2. See letter of 8 December 1944, n. 1.

3. José would probably have been reading *Transfigured Night* (New York: October House, 1946) or scattered poems of Vazakas appearing in *Hudson Review, Accent, Contemporary Poetry, Kenyon Review, Harper's*, and the *New York Times*.

4. *Marlborough: His Life and Times* (New York: Scribner's, 1933–38), 6 vols., a biography of John Churchill Marlborough, first duke of Marlborough (1650–1722).

5. R. P. Blackmur, "The Everlasting Effort: A Citation of T. E. Lawrence," in *The Expense of Greatness* (New York: Arrow Editions, 1940). Churchill's "frantic admiration" for Lawrence appeared at least once in an article entitled "Lawrence of Arabia: That Embarrassing Moment in the Royal Presence," *ExServices Association of Malaya Magazine* (Spring 1937): 19–24. Even Borges wrote on Lawrence for *Sur* in 1933.

drawing he made after seeing one of the old man's last pictures. It's really great. I wish you could see it. I was reading him the other day. I never could understand his dislike, intolerance absurd, for novelists. He detested V. Woolf, Lawrence, etc. And of Stendhal— well, he is interested in him as a type of intelligence!

Do write pronto and give me news of the other Continent

Pepe

[Hartford, Connecticut]
March 5, 1946

Dear José (if I may say so):

I put off replying to your recent letter until the copies of *Orígenes* came. Of course, I know nothing about Spanish and cannot even pronounce it decently; yet it seems to me that Mr. Felíu has caught my particular rhythm.[1] To me this seems to be particularly true in the last few verses of the last poem. I think it was Tasso who delighted to read Greek without having any knowledge whatsoever of that language. In the same way I take an even greater delight in reading my own poems in Spanish. Please thank Mr. Felíu for me.

I am enclosing a check for $15 to renew my subscription to *Orígenes* for a year or two and, in addition, to make it possible for you to send me a volume or two of Mr. Felíu's own poems the next time you are in Havana. No doubt there is a bookseller there who will take care of this for you. If there is a little money left, turn it over to the treasury.

You have asked about Byron Vazakas: His father was a professor of Greek at Columbia University. He lives, as it happens, in the same town in Pennsylvania where I lived as a boy.[2] I have met him and regard him as sensitive and intelligent, but the truth is that I read very little of other people's poetry.

Perhaps this will be of some interest to you, that lately I have read *A Naturalist in Cuba,* by Thomas Barbour.[3] Dr. Barbour died a month or two ago. He was in charge of the Botanical Institution at Soledad; he had many friends throughout Cuba, and not all of

1. See letter of 31 August 1945, n. 1.
2. Reading.
3. Boston: Little, Brown, 1945.

them scientists. For instance, the second chapter of the book that I have just finished is devoted to the restaurants in Havana. He enjoyed the cuisine of Cuba just as he enjoyed its cigars, particularly in more colossal sizes.

It is a curious experience to read poems like those that have just appeared in *Orígenes* after the lapse of six months or more from the time when they were written. We seem to be experiencing a rather violent change of taste. The misery of Europe, which was greater six months ago than it is now, seems not to have been so real to us then as it is now; and the more real it becomes the more sharply one feels that poetry of this sort is academic and unreal. One is inclined, therefore, to sympathize with one's more unsympathetic critics. It is all well enough to say that, in the long run, what was appropriate once will be appropriate again, but it does not follow; after all, nothing follows. The life of a poet, like the life of a painter, is just as difficult and unpredictable as the life of a speculator in Wall Street. But if a poet experiences these eras in which what he thinks and writes seems to be otiose, he is bound to recognize that in the same eras, almost everything that other people write, as well as the pictures they paint, and the music they write seems to be equally otiose. Yet to live exclusively in reality is as intolerable as it is incomprehensible, and I can say this even though yesterday, after playing a little Debussy on the gramophone, I thought how exactly he sounded like Chaminade.[4]

With many thanks to you and Mr. Felíu, I am

Very sincerely yours,
Wallace Stevens

San Miguel—March 21, 1946

My dear Wallace Stevens:

Thank you very much for your contribution to *Orígenes*. I am sorry I cannot send you anything published by Mr. Felíu. He has not published anything as yet. I will however tell him.

I am at the moment in San Miguel de los Baños—literally Saint Michael of the Baths—a health resort near Habana. Its mineral

4. Relative to Debussy's contribution as a composer, Chaminade's is so minor that this comic observation suggests a discerning musical ear.

waters are famous; they are very curative, especially for those who
suffer of liver and stomacal troubles. I am resting; there is nothing
here to distract one's life: no movies, parties, known people who
can pester us with their invitations, etc. It's a lovely little village,
surrounded by high lomas (hills). The vegetation is very puritanical
in appearance; mostly palm trees—no flowers. In the evening I meet
some of the town's capitans (that's how we call here the Chinese)
and play dominoes. It's very amusing to watch them play—they are
so calm and serious about everything. Sometimes we play billiards
and *asi* life rounds up the perfect day. I do nothing else; most of the
time I just sit and watch the modest citizens (really very poor)
walk about, selling lottery tickets or marching about the streets
with their sad-looking horses to incite some rich sick-visitor to take
a hike on horses and win therefore a few pesos.

I have been reading Joyce's *Ulysses* again. It's my only companion for the hours of meditation. I came across these wonderful
lines this morning—"that stony effigy in frozen music, horned and
terrible, of the human form divine, that eternal symbol of wisdom
and prophecy which, if aught that the imagination or the hand of
the sculptor has wrought in marble of soultransfigured and of soul-
transfiguring deserves to live, deserves to live."[1] Certainly, Joyce had
style! But at times he seems so old-fashioned, so demodé. I can tell
you that this village is most appropriate for the reading of *Ulysses:*
the vulgarity and common life there described equates with the
milieu that surrounds me. Although Joyce was extremely refined in
his manner of governing and manipulating *words,* indeed a musical
genius determined to make them dance to any tune he proposed,
there is in his works (his mind, too?) a vulgarity which I cannot
quite understand. It's most obvious when he is the perfect naturalist
writer, in those first chapters about L. Bloom, but even when he is
a symbolist, one finds the picture presented so marvelously (thru
the medium of words which here again thru incantation tends to
fool the reader) detestable. Perhaps, the most rewarding *effect* is the
metaphysical implications woven thru this common adventure.

But let me not bore you too much with an old theme. You must
know better than I what he pretended to portray. Yet, if some have

---

1. José is quoting from the Aeolus episide of *Ulysses.* The passage is a
description of Michelangelo's "Moses."

accused Joyce of obscurantism, I feel that it is his unnatural clarity
that confounds us at times.

Do write to my Habana address. I shall be returning anon. An
affectionate salute from your grateful friend,

Pepe or
José

La Habana
May 10, 1946

My dear and most kind friend:

All the admiration and longing for a more personal friendship
could be expressed by my telling you how delighted and grateful I
am to you. Reading, caressing (it almost comes to that) your marvelous "Esthétique" has been a benediction. What a perfectly bal-
anced little volume; what a delicate reunion of printing, drawing
and poetry![1] It comes to exclaiming that it is the most regaling
present I have ever received and from a poet I don't even know
personally. What a pity circumstances keep me so far away and pro-
hibit a more intimate colloquy! It was at dusk that I arrived from
San Miguel de los Baños and tore the carefully packed package and
in an atmosphere of roses and yellows and Uccello blues I perused
the book. I so wanted then to have you near and pour upon your
attentive ear the delight that infused me in that instant. Enough
that I have the poetry and the promise of a vision.

I am looking forward to seeing where you published the poems
you sent us originally for *Orígenes*.[2] Did you get my cable?

I am at present quite busy with *Orígenes,* Spring number. Soon
it will be on its way to Hartford. It contains my translation of "East
Coker" and "Pluies" of Perse.[3]

My brother and mother are leaving soon for New York. I remain
here as the watch-dog until they return. Then I am seriously considering going down to Buenos Aires to enter the Institute of Phi-

1. *Esthétique du Mal, a poem by Wallace Stevens,* with pen-and-ink
drawings by Wightman Williams (Cummington, Mass.: Cummington
Press, 1945).

2. "A Word With José Rodríguez-Feo" and "Paisant Chronicle" were
published in *Voices.*

3. *Orígenes* 3, no. 9 (Spring 1946): 21–27.

lology there, where I have a very dear friend: Pedro Henríquez Ureña whose *Literary Currents in Hispanic America* (his Charles Eliot Norton lectures) are published by Harvard University.[4]

I have seen the last issue of *View* (a silly Paris issue), *Partisan Review* (equally silly) and the *Sewanee* and *Kenyon*. It all makes me despair. The story that won the Bishop Prize was below high school standards. What is the matter with these people? The poetry that is appearing in all these magazines? Really, it comes to a very confusing melange of genres and academic, forgotten Parisian fashions. Even French literary production seems more vulgar and monotonous than ever before. Old Gide still fascinates me, but the rest . . . well, pooh as you once said of a fashionable surrealist clown.[5]

Do let me know of yourself and what you are doing in Hartford. Are the trees all green and the wild-flowers inciting young men into the woods?

Your furriously admiring Antillean,
José

[Hartford, Connecticut]
May 21, 1946

Dear Antillean:

This is merely to say how much pleasure your letter of May 10th has given me. I passed along a part of it to the printer of the book because printers who are as good as this one deserve to hear sympathetic comment.[1]

4. See Introduction, p. 7.

5. The "fashionable surrealist clown" is Charles Henri Ford, editor of *View;* see letters of 14 and 20 June 1945. The "Paris issue" of Ford's magazine (vol. 6, nos. 2 and 3, March–April 1946) included a full-page photograph of André Gide by Cecil Beaton, bearing the caption "Over seventy and still in the vanguard of French literature." José read the all-French issue of *Partisan Review* 8, no. 2 (Spring 1946). And the spring issue of the *Kenyon Review* (vol. 8, no. 2) contained Gide's essay on Valéry. Some years later, however, José's estimation of Gide fell sharply; see letter of 25 February 1952.

1. On 14 May Stevens quoted phrases from José's letter of 10 May to the printer, Harry Duncan; see *L,* 528, n. 5 (HS).

The Four Poems will appear in *Voices*[2] in the late autumn. I shall send you a copy. When I sent the poems to them, I told them that they had been printed in *Orígenes* and I gave them enough information to make it possible for them to say something about it. What they will do remains to be seen. *Voices* is a little off my circuit. But perhaps it does one more good to appear a little off one's circuit than merely to go round and round and round. It is a little like adverse critcism which always does one more good than the highly favorable kind of thing.

I am looking forward to a visit to Boston in early June. My class at Harvard is holding a reunion. Although I have never gone in for reunions, there is a special reason for making an exception this year and because of that reason I have agreed to turn up at a clam bake in Scituate. The truth is that the only other clam bake that I have ever been to was my idea of a poor picnic. However, the one at Scituate may be different.

Yours very truly,
Wallace Stevens

[Hartford, Connecticut]
August 13, 1946

Dear José:

A day or two ago, I read in the *New York Times* that one of our eminent war profiteers[1] had been found at the Club Kawama at Varadero. On that very day, I received your letter from that particular spot, which I had never heard of before. But then, Cuba is full of places that I have never heard of before and shall never see.

I am delighted to hear that you are planning to be in New York around September 18th. We are going down to Pennsylvania on August 30th and will be there about ten days or two weeks and we may be drifting home through New York. If you know where you

2. The four poems had originally appeared in *Orígenes;* see letter of 31 August 1945, n. 1.

1. As Murray Garsson's $78 million in war contracts were being examined by the Senate War Investigation Committee, Garsson dodged reporters for a week by living under an asumed name at the Kawama Club at Varadero.

are going to stop and let me know, I should be glad to try to find you. But if you do not know, then you can send word to Hartford after your arrival, and I shall come down.

About this time of year, I am double my normal size, what with Corn-on-the-Cob, Blueberries, and so on. Perhaps I shall be eating triple before long, because we have been having all the butter we want recently. However, the primaries will soon be over. It may be that after that important political feature of our lives is behind us, butter will be rationed again until just before Christmas.[2] We begin to take politics not as having anything to do with the Government of ourselves, but as a rather tiring game for the superficial.

It would be interesting to talk with you about what you call our loss of interest in the beauty of Nature, but it would be most interesting to talk to you about the eccentricities that ensue. I wonder whether you are right about outgrowing nature. Perhaps the man who has never had a chance to enjoy life, outgrows it. One of my firm beliefs is that Life and Nature are one. Consequences of boredom are, therefore, practically unknown to me. Perhaps I have been bored at Church, or at the Theatre, or by a book, but certainly, I have never been bored in any general sense and at my ripe age, I am quite sure that I never shall be. The extent to which Nature and Life are the same, is something on which you ought to be able to throw a particular light, because you have the advantage of all your wonderful beaches.

I look forward to seeing you,

Very sincerely yours,
Wallace Stevens

An eccentric stenographer explains many things about this letter, paper, etc.[3]

2. A good many of the senators and representatives who were up for reelection in November faced challenges from the right in primaries within their parties. By the time José received this letter, the big news was the defeat of incumbent Senator Robert M. LaFollette, Jr., of Wisconsin, who lost in a primary to thirty-six-year-old Circuit Judge Joseph McCarthy.

3. This postscript is handwritten. The only thing "eccentric" about the letter is apparently the paper. All other letters to José were typewritten on company letterhead; this was not.

[Middlebury, Vermont]
August 25, 1946

My dear Mr. Stevens:

It might surprise you to hear from this old and forgetful monster. I have been sojourning in Vermont, where my liver has turned for the better and it all makes me very cheerful and hopeful. I assisted the Middlebury Spanish School; roamed around with old Spanish friends; read a great deal and wrote several essays and short stories, besides translating several pieces for *Orígenes.*

I suppose you are now in Chester, vacationing. I hope anyways you will let me know exactly where you will be during the first week of September. I am going to Boston next week; then I shall motor to N.Y. so if you are at home, I will stop and have a cocktail with you. If you are in Chester, I might come up there, for I shall not stop in N.Y. but go on directly to Baltimore where I am going to stay with some friends for two weeks.

Of course, there is lots to tell, but I should rather wait until I see you once more.

Write me as soon as you receive this letter, to Box 95, Middlebury, Vermont.

Yours devotedly,
José Rodríguez-Feo

[Middlebury, Vermont]
August 27, [1946]

My dear prisoner of Hartford:

My writings are slow like a silken thread tracing its alphabet on a deserted mosaic; but I escape the tedious highball and the company of plumed ladies to proclaim the uniqueness of my schedules. If I enter the city of Hartford, it shall be at exactly noon so as to trap the poet as he exits from the walled citadel of the insurances. I must then remain in Boston, clock in hand, waiting for the salvo from the Spanish culebrine which will send me off in a race against Time. Imagine what would occur if I were to be delayed in my schedule. I would find you gone; lost for three quarters of an hour. I am motoring; but I shall detail precisely the route so as not to confirm the old Gothic invention of mañana and retarded overtures.

What a triumph; to immortalize with the twelve bells the fame of my timeliness.

I have been reading Pound and Babbitt; they all have a queer flavour now. And we only relish their peculiar, amusing impatience with their times which is our peculiar, amusing impatience with our times. You might like to learn that your favorite designer of pine-apples (I am thinking now of that famous poem on the pineapple where you allude to the cone and to Cuba)[1] is coming soon to the Metropolis.

Let me finish by saying that your lovely ties now adorn my strolls around the trails of Vermont.

Yours sincerely

José

[Hartford, Connecticut]

October 2, 1946

Dear José:

We left Hartford on August 30th expecting to be back home at the end of two weeks. At that time it was my understanding that you would be in New York about September 17th and I planned to run down to New York to see you. As a matter of fact, we stayed more than three weeks in Hershey where we had one of the happiest holidays we have ever had. After that we went to Reading for several days. Actually, we were back in New York on Tuesday, September 24th the day after you left. I called up the Stanhope, which confirmed your departure. We thought that we should stay in New York until the end of the week but it was impossible to find any satisfactory accommodations. The long and short of it is that we came back to Hartford without staying in New York at all.

---

1. "Someone Puts a Pineapple Together" is the only poem José could be referring to. Evidently Stevens sent a version of it to José, or perhaps to Mariano himself, the "designer of pineapples," six months before its first public appearance in a lecture at Harvard in February 1947. The poem was published with "Of Ideal Time and Choice" and the essay "The Realm of Resemblance" in *Partisan Review* 14 (May 1947): 243–53. When Stevens told José at the end of the year of his upcoming lecture at Harvard and noted that as yet "I am only thinking about my subject," he was apparently referring to the essay; see the letter of 19 December 1946.

It is unnecessary to say that I am terribly sorry about this. Even our telephone conversation amounted to nothing because I could not hear you. The telephone connection in my room was a good connection but it was just my luck that when you called I was not in my room. You said something about a book of about twenty-five pages. If you would like to write to me about this, I should be glad to be of any possible service to you, but what I have just said is absolutely all that I heard and I have not the faintest idea, therefore, of what you had in mind. Do, please, forgive me for all this. But, after all, we had one of the happiest times of our lives and it sounded very much as if you were enjoying New York. The good in what happened outweighs the evil.

Perhaps you will be back in Havana by the time this arrives there, particularly if you are not staying in Mexico City any longer than you stayed in New York. Please write me so that I may be sure that you were not offended. There is so much to do during these first days back in the office that I shall have to put off writing to you in a more leisurely way until a little later on.

With my very best regards, I am

Sincerely yours,
Wallace Stevens

[Havana]
November 30, 1946

My dear friend:

On my return from Mexico City I found your lamenting letter; also that wonderful series of poems you published in the *Quarterly Review of Literature* in New Haven. There! I was surprised, and so pleased!, to see one commemorating my old bath resort: San Miguel de los Baños.[1] How very fine of you, to pay homage to our

---

1. The following poems, collected under the title "More Poems for Liadoff," appeared in the *Quarterly Review of Literature* 3 (Fall 1946): "A Woman Sings a Song for a Soldier Come Home," "The Pediment of Appearance," "Burghers of Petty Death," "Human Arrangement," "A Good Man Has No Shape," "The Red Fern," "A Packet of Anacharsis," "The Dove in the Belly," "Mountains of Cats," "The Prejudice against the Past," "Extraordinary References," and "Attempt to Discover Life," the poem about José's "old bath resort."

little local villages. And that vision of the "cadaverous person"; how magical the discovery![2] How come you see from so far-off those touching scenes? I have translated the poem and propose it to be included in this Winter issue. But tell me what are Hermosas?

Mexico was delightfully primitive, not in Lawrence proportion, and full of intellectual activity. Its writers and poets are very kind to newcomers, full of questions and sympathy. I left New York because I couldn't stand its dismal people and there were no concerts, no good plays. And then missing you was such a disappointment. But I expect to return soon. My brother, Orlando, is living on Long Island with his American wife. He has just been blessed with an infant so I don't know if he can put me up. I am awaiting his answer. If I can't go, I shall take a trip to Caracas, Venezuela. A very dear friend of mine, the music critic, Alejo Carpentier, has invited me over. He has just published a wonderful book on the history of our music: *La Música en Cuba*.[3] Did you have a chance to see Mariano's exhibition in New York? Did you read Elizabeth Bishop's new book of poetry?[4] What did you think of Williams' *Paterson 1?* By the way Harvard's *Bulletin* tells me you have been awarded a poetry prize.[5] Felicitations!! There I had a chance to see your likeness. It wasn't a very good picture, I guess.

My life flows as usual. I write, read and frequent the company of a few and selected amigos. I am as lonely as ever and yet quite happy in my isolation. All the vines are in bloom now, and looking across its flowery branches I see the sky remains blue and shining up there. What more can you ask of life? To open one's eyes in the morning and see only flowers and the open spaces blue and white above. And to read kind, friendly messages from our friends below. It doesn't signify that we avert suffering and misery, all that is within us, but we must remain platonic and make the best of the little things the gods so kindly offer us every day: be it the vision of a violet bouganville or the song of a banana vendor. I think that is

2. *CP,* 370, line 8.
3. Mexico: Fund for Economic Culture, 1946.
4. *North and South* (Boston: Houghton Mifflin, 1946).
5. In June Stevens had learned from the president of the University of Chicago that he was being awarded the Harriet Monroe Poetry Award for 1946.

wisdom, not cowardice. I prefer to be foolish in those little things; not be made a fool reaching for the stars.

My dear and kind friend, please forgive the long silence. It only means I was preoccupied with other things. Yet there is always a warm and affectionate embrace for my Hartford poet.

> Yours sincerely,
> José

[Hartford, Connecticut]
December 10, 1946

Dear José:

I am glad to have your letter. Although I don't intend to reply to it today, perhaps I ought to explain Hermosas, which are a variety of roses. Of course, I don't know that Hermosas grow at San Miguel. But, then, probably nobody else knows. Besides, the San Miguel of the poem is a spiritual not a physical place. The question that is prompted by that poem is whether the experience of life is in the end worth more than tuppence: dos centavos. I shall write to you again when I have a little more time. I enjoy writing to you and hearing from you.

> Very truly yours,
> Wallace Stevens

[Hartford, Connecticut]
December 19, 1946

Dear José:

When I wrote to you the other day I did not have time to talk about a number of things.

A friend of mine once told me that there was considerable difference between the Spanish spoken in Mexico and Spanish spoken in Cuba. He thought Spanish spoken in Mexico more academically correct. How did it strike you? During the last several years I have been taking a number of Mexican magazines. In the last week or two I have discontinued my subscription to *Cuadernos Americanos*.[1]

---

1. *Cuadernos Americanos* began publication in 1942 in Mexico under the editorship of Jesus Silva Herzog.

It is an extraordinary publication but it overwhelms me. As I take it merely in order to read a little Spanish now and then, I can glut myself on back numbers and, therefore, need not continue to take it.

One great difficulty about everything Mexican is the appalling interest in the Indians: the Mayas, and so on. It is just as if every time one picked up a number of the *New Yorker* one found a dozen illustrations of life among the early Dutch settlers. After all, few writers tell us what we really want to know about the Indians. One sees pictures of the Mayas, and this, that and the other. These things never take one below the surface and I have yet to feel about any Maya that he was made of clay. Publications like *Cuadernos Americanos* convince one that he was made of putty.

What you say about New York is interesting because it reflects my own reaction. It is very dull there now. As I am a good deal older than you are apparently, I am quite sure that it is not going to stay that way. During the first World War when we were cut off from Europe and had to get along on American books and American art, we had a situation very much like the present situation. I don't mean to say anything dismal about American books and American art. What I do mean to say is that people who are interested in such things are insatiable and want, in addition, English books and English art, French books and French art, and so on. It is like being confined to a metropolis without access to a dozen others. It just does not work.

And, by the way, I did not see Mariano's show. I knew of it. What I have just been speaking of is one reason why I did not see it. When there is no good reason to go to New York, I don't go and, in reality, only business takes me there. Yesterday I went down to attend a meeting in the afternoon and in the morning I went to the Morgan Library where they are holding an exhibition of Missals, Breviaries, Books of Hours, etc., most of them on vellum and most of them very early 12th and 13th century English, French, Italian and Spanish. The exhibition is typical of the great wealth of the Morgan Library. I spent an hour there although I could have spent a day. The illuminations in the Spanish manuscripts are exquisitely and dramatically done, yet they meant less than the early French manuscripts because there is a primitiveness and a perfection about most early French things beyond comparison with anything else.

One reason why I went to New York was to see my eye doctor. At my age trouble with one's eyes is rather frightening. In fact, most such things are important, not for what they are, but as symptoms. As it turned out, there was nothing serious the matter but the doctor thought that I ought very much to cut down my reading and not read at night, which, after all, is the only time when I do read, and not to drink coffee, which I never touch, and not to drink anything alcoholic, which I rarely do. But I have been expecting something of this sort for a long time and have been reading less and less.

I know Miss Bishop's work. She lives in Key West. And, of course, Williams[2] is an old friend of mine. I have not read *Paterson.* I have the greatest respect for him, although there is the constant difficulty that he is more interested in the way of saying things than in what he has to say. The fact remains that we are always fundamentally interested in what a writer has to say. When we are sure of that, we pay attention to the way in which he says it, not often before.

Have I told you that I am going to lecture at Harvard in February?[3] On this occasion I am only thinking about my subject: not reading about it. I am not going to quote anybody. Taking a new and rather quackish subject and developing it without the support of others is not quite the easiest thing in the world to do. If, however, I get nowhere with it, I can always abandon it and do something else. It is curious how a subject once chosen grows like a beanstalk until it seems as if there had never been anything else in the world.

I love the little vistas of Cuba that you put in your letters.

Merry Christmas and a Happy New Year. How do you say that in Spanish? I should be much at home in Caracas because I believe that many of the birds that spend their summers in Hartford spend their winters in Caracas.

Always, sincerely yours,
Wallace Stevens

2. Stevens' eyesight was sharp enough on this day to catch his (or his stenographer's) significant error: initially the name read "Hugh Williams." Houghton Library manuscript, Harvard University.

3. "Three Academic Pieces," *NA,* 71–89.

[Havana]
December 19 [1946]

My dear Poeta:

It was wonderful to have the *cartero* (the mailman) who is very
black and has beautiful white teeth hand me two letters from Hartford. It came at the right moment; I was feeling so miserable with
my liver in revolt and my colon all irritated through some misterious
intoxications and the doctor piping all night "you must go north
to the cold weather, it will cure you, it will cure you"; it was such
a lovely letter! Your provocative words on Mexicans are quite correct: in my last trip the constant preoccupation of all my artistic
companions were the poor, exploited Indians; they are not of clay
however and seemed to inhabit their imaginations in a very curious
fashion. Out of it all have come beautiful books like *Montezuma,
el de la silla de oro* of that very fine prosist, Francisco Monterde and
the poems and stories of Ali Chumacero.[1] And the great drawings
recently exhibited in Cuidad de Mexico by Orozco and those marvelous murals of Rivera. How amazing that we should coincide in
so many things! *Cuadernos* overwhelms me too. Don't you receive
El Hijo Prodigo,[2] edited by the poet, Xavier Villaurrutia? It's the
best Mexican literary review and always has lovely reproductions
to gaze at if you do not care to strain your eyes too much.

I have been reading an amazing book: *William Blake: The
Politics of Vision*[3] by Mr. Mark Schorer. It is the best book I have
perused on Blake, a figure much to my heart. It is very academic,
in a way, very learned, full of quotes, and permeated by that pro-
fessorial scent so dear to all who have taken a promenade through
dear old Widener. His discussion of mysticism is very sane and
competent; many of our modern writers should read them so that
we won't be bombarded with such nonsense as we read in their
books nowadays. He has delicious sayings like "As his work ap-
proaches its end, his obscurity increases not at all because he is
becoming more mystical, but because he is becoming more per-

1. The same Mexican publisher, Imprenta Universitaria, issued Monterde's book in 1945 and Chumacero's *Páramo de sueños* in 1944.
2. *El Hijo Pródigo: Revista literaria* began publishing in Mexico in 1943.
3. New York: H. Holt and Company, 1946.

verse." Something quite new and yet so true of the artist: his perversity. And the critics have seldom noticed this trait in their conduct. Reading the Marquis of Sade I noticed that lately not so much the perversity of things described, as the perversity of style, his taking so much pain to be very literary about it. And of course I have always believed that the greatest poets are those who can best employ the artifices of literature and those simplicities of style [that] are at the bottom so artificial! Of course, the mystic is in disaccord with the poet and Mr. Schorer puts it very well: "Mysticism in its highest moment is without images or symbols, it is entirely *non-sensory,* just as it is without ideas that relate to nature." Thus we can well say that even St. John of the Cross was not a mystic poet, but was a mystic who wrote the most perfect poetry of the Spanish language. I think Maritain has said something quite similar, somewhere. Schorer's discussions of why Protestantism has not produced a mystic are quite relevant too; he says that "the mood of mysticism is everywhere in the history of P. but it is nearly impossible to find a mystic." And to close this report on Schorer's book let me quote this passage which I am sure will interest you greatly: "Myths are the instruments by which we continually struggle to make our experience intelligible to ourselves. A myth is a large, controlling image that gives philosophical meaning to the facts of life; that is, which has organizing value for experience. A mythology is a more or less articulated body of such images, a pantheon. Without such images, experience is chaotic, fragmentary and merely phenomenal. It is the chaos of experience that creates them, and they are intended to rectify it. All real conviction involved a mythology, either in its usual, broad sense or in a private sense." p. 27-28. I think that is something to think about when we come to examine modern literature. We can indeed speak of their failure to create a myth.

What you say of Williams is quite true. I find his *Paterson* the best example of that constant preoccupation with how to say things in a new manner. He told me that himself one day I visited him in New Jersey. He was obsessed with finding an American rhythm, and thus to describe the American scene in a new language. Also, he is a man of diverse complexions and had as I could see an almost envious admiration of T. S. Eliot. But I like his poetry and find some pleasure in reading it; something I cannot say for everyone else. I was reading yesterday Henry Treece[4] and couldn't get to the end without feeling very bored and quite fatigued. Maybe my dominion of the language is softening, and I cannot enjoy now the more intricate poetry being written. And yet, I had such fun reading *The Sacred Fount* of James with its never-ending, comic situations and conversations to baffle the most remarkable linguists.

I am glad you are going to old Harvard in February. As I told you it is possible I should go to New York next month; then perhaps I might even assist to your conference. I don't know what to make of your rather sarcastic remark "I know Miss Bishop's work. She lives in Key West." And nothing more on that topic.

Your poem, with the Hermosas too, will appear in the Winter issue of *Orígenes*. Do you believe that "the experience of life is in the end worth more than dos centavos"?

Write soon. *Felices Pascuas y Un Prospero Año Nuevo.*

Truly yours,
José

At 5 PM on 20 March, at the Ritz Tower, 57th Street and Park Avenue, New York City, Stevens and José met for the first time. "I invited him to have dinner with me," Stevens wrote Henry Church, "but have told him that I shall have to leave at 7:30 to catch the eight o'clock train for Hartford" (*L,* 550). Stevens wanted to see Church also on the twentieth, and invited Church to join him and José; "I have never met him and have no idea what he is like," he warned Church. "He may be all teeth and no ears." Apparently Stevens and Church met at another time and place that day; it was the last time they saw each other (Church died on 4 April).

José was visiting the United States for a few weeks, partly to arrange his graduate program at Princeton. He must have mentioned his plans for enrolling at Princeton to Stevens on the twentieth; when they met again on Monday, 7 April, for lunch and drinks at the Ritz, Allen Tate, of Princeton, joined them. When inviting Tate, Stevens wrote, "[José] is likeable personally and would enjoy meet-

4. José was probably reading Treece's *Collected Poems* (New York: Knopf, 1946) or perhaps his volume *The Black Seasons* (London: Faber and Faber, 1945).

ing you, I think. If you know of anyone who would be interested in
meeting him, bring him along." Stevens also took the opportunity
to decline Tate's plea for him to record a reading of poems for the
Library of Congress, commenting, "I think that I ought to say so
now so that you can devote yourself to the life and letters of Havana
and Hartford" (*L,* 551).

Stevens' next letter indicates that José returned to Havana but
made plans to return to New York during the summer. The letter
also indicates that at least one letter or card has been lost.]

[Hartford, Connecticut]
May 23, 1947

Dear José:

Hartford was never lovelier than it is right now, notwithstanding
all the rain, most of which comes from Quebec and back of Quebec.
I shall bear in mind that you will be at the Berkshire, but I am not
at all sure it will be possible for me to be in New York during your
stay. I hope so.

I was in New York last week and had dinner with the editors of
the *Partisan Review.*[1] One of them told me that Eliot's brother had
just died. He had come over to this country, I believe, for the purpose of being with his brother. I know nothing about his family,
but, since he is said to have several sisters, the death of his brother
with whom the sisters lived probably makes it necessary for him to
take over to some extent.[2] I did not see *Time* magazine, but from
what you say gather that someone has taken a crack at Eliot.[3] Some-

1. William Phillips, Philip Rahv, Delmore Schwartz, and William Bar-
rett; Stevens' "Three Academic Pieces" appeared in the May–June issue
of *Partisan Review.*

2. Eliot had flown to New York on 22 April to be with his brother,
Henry, who died twelve days later. Eliot spent two months in the United
States winding up Henry's affairs.

3. An essay in the book section of the 19 May issue of *Time,* entitled
"Milton Is O.K.," made light of Eliot's delivery of "a new lecture on an
old enemy." A photo of Eliot gripping his lapels bore the one-word caption: "Obligation." The lecture on Milton took place on 3 May at the
Frick Museum and José was in the audience. José met up with Eliot after
the lecture at the Oak Room of the Plaza Hotel, where they "got on fine"

one takes a crack at everybody sooner or later: not only at everybody but at everything. In the long run, as Poe said in one of his essays which nobody reads, the generous man comes to be regarded as the stingy man; the beautiful woman comes to be regarded as an old witch; the scholar becomes the ignoramus.[4] The hell with all this. For my own part I like to live in a classic atmosphere, full of my own gods and to be true to them until I have some better authority than a merely contrary opinion for not being true to them. We have all to learn to hold fast.

Yours very truly,
Wallace Stevens

Nov. 25, 1947
Cambridge, Mass.

Dear Mr. Stevens:

I know you're wondering as to my whereabouts. I am sorry I've kept so quiet. I shall motor back to N.Y. next Friday, and hope to phone you if I get to Hartford before 12 a.m. Otherwise I shall be at the Stanhope Hotel, 81st and Fifth Avenue Fri–thru Mon.

I came to see Amado Alonso,[1] the Spanish scholar, teaching at Harvard now on the old issue of coming back to obtain my Ph.D.

There have been a series of lectures on Cervantes (excuse: the Centenary). Mr. Levin (Harry) spoke on Cervantes and Melville; Mr. W. H. Auden will close the series with the topic The Ironic Hero on Dec. 3.

Please write and let me know whether you shall be coming to N.Y. before Dec. 9. I am going to Princeton on Dec. 1 and back to Habana on the 9th.

Yours sincerely,
José Rodríguez Feo

---

after three martinis. Eliot gave José permission to translate two of the *Four Quartets* for *Orígenes*. Letter from José Rodríguez Feo to Alan Filreis, 26 April 1983.

4. The paraphrase has not been identified as having a source in Poe.

1. d. 1952. Alonso founded and edited the monumental *Biblioteca de Dialectologia Hispanoamericana* and other series of philological studies.

[Hartford, Connecticut]
November 28, 1947

Dear José:

I am going to be in New York on December 8th in the afternoon and also on the 9th the greater part of the day. I shall have some appointments and have a date for the evening of December 8th. I think it would be best to leave it this way: I shall call you up at the Stanhope at some time when I think you are likely to be there: morning or evening.

It was nice to hear from you, particularly since I thought you were lying in a hammock on some piazza in Cuba, sore about my lack of hospitality, as to which I was helpless.

Sincerely yours,
Wallace Stevens

José Rodríguez Feo in 1948.

Wallace Stevens on the steps of the Hartford Accident and Indemnity
Company, Summer 1952. (Photo, © Rollie McKenna)

ORIGENES

REVISTA DE ARTE Y LITERATURA

LA HABANA   *Primavera*   1 9 1 1

Cover of the first issue of *Orígenes* (Spring 1944), line drawing by
Mariano Rodríguez.

ORIGENES

REVISTA DE ARTE Y LITERATURA

LA HABANA   *Verano*   1 9 4 4

Cover of *Orígenes* 1, no. 2 (Summer 1944), line drawing by Mariano Rodríguez.

ORIGENES
Calle B No. 156
Reparto Almendares
La Habana, Cuba

Jan—
Feb. 23, 1951

My dear Wallachio:

Excuse this prolongued silence.
I haven't been well. I had just been
operated in the throat. And now I am
getting ready for the apendicitis operation.
So if I see you in March (as I hope), I
shall be a 'new' man. Even the tone of
my voice will be new, fresh.

I finally sent for a Primitive
the poem I asked you about. Gotham
Book Mart will send it along soon.

I also sent for ticket for The
Cocktail Party which I saw advertise
in a New Yorker here. So you see
I am planning an escape very, very
soon, my dear friend. And yet
I am very contented here; I am
pondering seriously the idea of
forgeting the claustros of Princeton
or Harvard & settling down again.

Holograph letter from José Rodríguez Feo to Wallace Stevens, 23
January 1951. (Reproduced by permission of the Huntington Library,
San Marino, California)

Cut-out of Pluto, used by Stevens to simulate a commercial sympathy card, sent to José in November 1948. See p. 141. (By permission of Holly Stevens and the Houghton Library, Cambridge, Massachusetts)

Reading of Orígenes (1944), oil painting by Mariano Rodríguez, re-produced in *Orígenes* 1, no. 3 (October 1945). (Courtesy, National Museum of Art, Havana, Cuba. Photo by Raidel Chao)

Orígenes Group photographed in the church of Father Angel Gaztelu, a poet and member of the group. *Standing, left to right:* Cintio Vitier, Mariano Rodríguez, Alfredo Lozano, José Lezama Lima, Lorenzo García Vega, Mario Parajón, Julián Orbón, Gastón Baquero, Aracely Zambrano, Enrique Labrador Ruiz, Augustín Pí. *Seated, left to right:* Mercedis Orbón, Fiña García Marruz, Father Angel Gaztelu, Maria Zambrano, José Rodríguez Feo. (From Lorenzo García Vega, *Los Años de Orígenes* [Caracas, Venezuela: Monte Avila Editores, 1978])

DEAR OLD PRINCETON

1948–1949

Despite numerous attempts to get together, Stevens and José met only a few times during the two years José was in and out of the Spanish doctoral program at Princeton University. He left for Cuba during the 1947–48 academic year because of his mother's illness, returning in September 1948 to begin work as a graduate instructor. A meeting confirmed by their letters, that of 18 April 1949 in Manhattan, was significant: José gave Stevens Santayana's letter and asked Stevens if he would write a letter of introduction to Alfred Knopf (which he never used, perhaps because it was so understated and noncommittal). They dined and then took a walking tour of several of Stevens' favorite delicatessens and fruiteries ("I realized then that to him a piece of fruit was more than something to eat," José recalls. "It was good enough for him to look at it and think about it").

Bananas, sapodillas, and pineapples "a foot high with spines fit to stick in the helmet of a wild chieftain" are essential to the letters of this period, even though much of the time both men were digging themselves out of Middle Atlantic snowstorms. Indeed, some of José's best anecdotes about Cuba are written from his rooms at Princeton: the Gothic tale of vengeful Consuelo is told here; so is the story of the Argentine that became "The Novel" during José's third semester. That José sorely missed Cuba and felt ostracized in a place where passion seemed subject to decorum and "even spring behaves" is obvious from the intensity with which his letters tell

these tales. At his most self-conscious ("I must close, feeling I have
given you a tip for a wonderful poem"), José realized the extent
to which *Stevens* initiated these things.

But the Ph.D. student did involve himself in the academic life.
He attended lectures by Jacques Maritain, had several good talks
with Spender and some near-misses with Eliot, survived a run-in
with Suzanne Langer, and enjoyed frequent contact with R. P.
Blackmur. Blackmur loved the anecdote about the Argentine and
repeated it to his colleagues. He was intrigued by the development
of "The Novel" from José's narrative to Stevens' meditation. Blackmur had long demonstrated his interest in the creative process of
which his student-friend was now a part. In "Examples of Wallace
Stevens" he had analyzed Stevens' use of nondramatic, meditative
verse to carry "real substance" in poetry. And in "An Abstraction
Blooded" he focused on the stages of a poetic idea; a supreme
fiction must refer to and somehow still *initiate* a story or scene,
which when transformed—abstracted, changed, and made pleasur-
able—becomes myth, miraculously removed from its source. When
José, with his direct experience, and Blackmur, with his theoretical
assumptions, sat down to examine the formation of Stevens' poems,
they learned still more about how quickly and fully removed from
their actual source José's words and stories became once he posted
them to Hartford. José adjusted to it, but he still "blushed" when
he saw how his phrases gave pleasure to the man who so often
denied it in himself.

[Hartford, Connecticut]
December 15, 1947

Dear José:

I called the Stanhope when I was in New York last week without result which was just as well because I had a lot of things to do.

[R. P.] Blackmur is, I take it, a Scot at bottom. Since I had a
Scotch grandmother, I am to that extent also a Scot. We have never
quite hit it off because that sort of thing takes time between people
who are not altogether on the surface. Then, too, in Blackmur's case
I told him a story about Frost several times when even the first time
seemed once too many. He is desperately devoted to everything in

which I am interested and I wish we were better friends. My last contact with him was in relation to something which in the long run has meant a great deal of money to the *Kenyon Review*. I am going to have a set of poems in the next number of the *Kenyon Review* and I expect that I shall receive from the source within the next month or so a prodigious check, which, after all, I shall owe to Blackmur and his associates.[1]

I am glad to know that you are to remain in Princeton. We expect to stay here in Hartford over the holiday although I have been telling people that we were going away. Grind away at your work for a while. I shall look forward to seeing you a little later on.

Sincerely yours,
Wallace Stevens

1. R. P. Blackmur was an advisory editor of the *Kenyon Review*, which published the "set of poems," "The Auroras of Autumn," in its winter issue, volume 10 (1948), 1–10. Stevens' "last contact" with Blackmur had been a year earlier, when Blackmur, Malcolm Cowley, and Lionel Trilling sent Stevens and other poets a questionnaire about the importance of American little magazines, implicitly a plea for financial support. Stevens refused to get involved and argued at length that it would be impossible to raise enough money to support even the worthy magazines. "Who is going to contribute on such a scale to such a project?" he asked Blackmur. Explaining voluntarism as an ideal, he cited *Cuadernos Americanos* ("far better than anything here, emerges with quality and elegance and regularity from the poverty of Mexico City") and *Orígenes* ("never sure of its next number, is the work of a loyal group in Havana"). Stevens to Blackmur, 4 November 1946, Blackmur Papers, Princeton University Library. He wrote again a week later, suggesting that the *Partisan Review*, "the best thing we have," would be worthy of support because "it is free from the academic associations" of the *Kenyon Review* and the *Sewanee Review*. Stevens to Blackmur, 12 November 1946. Despite this jab at Blackmur's own academic associations—probably also aimed at those of Tate and J. C. Ransom—Stevens' letter to José indicates that in the year following Blackmur's appeal, Stevens arranged for a "prodigious check," perhaps from Barbara Church, whose late husband, Henry, had once given the *Kenyon Review* $500. Henry Church to Allen Tate, 15 May 1943, Tate Papers, Princeton University Library.

Peacock Inn
Twenty Bayard Lane
Princeton, N. J.
Jan. 8 [1948]

My dear Mr. Stevens:

Hope you are well and enjoying this delightful weather! I was snow-bound for 4 days on Long Island over the Xmas holiday, when we had the Great Storm. I shall never forget it as long as I live. I would prefer a nice typhoon any month.

In N.Y. I had the pleasure of meeting Mr. Stephen Spender. He's a big, tall, lanky English-man, who looks very much the gentleman-image I fondly nestle in my mind for future reference and comparison to that day when I shall visit England. He speaks softly, with a lovely accent (Oxford?) and was very kind to me. He gave me his last poem, "Returning to Vienna", just printed by the Banyan Press. I hope to put it into some sort of decent Spanish for our original little review.[1] I have read lately Mr. V. S. Pritchett's *The Living Novel*[2] (he's an English-man too). A most delightful, witty sensible discussion of some forgotten novelists and little-read novels. You must look him (or it) up. Then I started *The Memoirs of St. Simon on the Reign of Louis XIV and the Regency*[3] which I have always wanted to look into, ever since dear old Proust mentioned it so enthusiastically. Now I see where the old boy picked up his craze for nobles, titles and courtly gossip. *The Memoirs* are the most highly seasoned and worldly of histories. I wish I could copy for you his description of Louis XIV's dismissal of Racine by poor Abbe Fenelon's disputations with Madame Maintenon and the Jesuits, on the death of Madame de Sévigné, etc. But, I know. You only read poetry, now, and I am afraid you'll never peruse it at all!

I led a very secluded life in N.Y. over the holiday. Didn't go to theaters or the music-halls. I did see the wonderful *Volpone,* with H[arry] Baur and L. Jouve, and peeked in again at the marvelous French tapestries. By the way, the Bracque exhibition opened last Monday in Rosenberg. I am going to N.Y. tomorrow to see my

1. It appeared in *Orígenes* 5, no. 17 (Spring 1948).
2. London: Chatto and Windus, 1946.
3. Translated by Bayle St. John in three volumes (London, 1876).

doctor and will go up to see Bracque's new things in the afternoon.

I am very contented in dear old Princeton. I am engrossed in my German language; read a great deal of Spanish literature and English. I finished *The Age of Anxiety* which made [me] very anxious as to the probable poetic course of Mr. Auden.[4] I thought the little book a frightful bore. Why must all the old poets go in for sermons? It was a rather sad day when they all discovered Kierkegaard! Later I re-read some of Wordsworth's beautiful poems and found him much more palatable.

I shall be in N.Y. until Monday the 12th for on that day my sister Olga arrives from Habana. Then I will return to my Peacock Inn for the rest of January. You can write me to the Peacock Inn.

Hope we can get together soon in New York. Just let me know when you are going to be there and are not to be in the St. Nicholas' banquets, etc.[5] I am ever devotedly

Yours—
José

[Hartford, Connecticut]
January 22, 1948

Dear José:

[V. S.] Pritchett of whom you speak in your last letter is a more or less regular contributor to *The Statesman,* of which I have been a reader from #1. He has a little story or apologue in a recent number which I am sending you separately. This tells about a person living in Italy who had been the subject of a number of stories and who in the end avenged himself by telling stories about the authors.[1]

4. The book is subtitled *A Baroque Eclogue* (New York: Random House, 1947).

5. Beginning in 1944, Stevens attended the annual dinners of the Saint Nicholas Society, a genealogical club for families of Dutch ancestry. A few years later, Stevens invited his Cuban friend to join him at one of these dinners; see Stevens' letter of 14 March 1949. Undoubtedly Stevens' Christmas card, which has not been found, indicated his attendance at the 1947 dinner.

1. Although the locale is Spain, Stevens is undoubtedly referring to V. S. Pritchett, "The Doctor's Story," *New Statesman and Nation* 35 (3 January 1948): 8–9.

I send it to you because you are becoming so literary that you ought
to understand that life fights back and that it will get you even on
the top floor of the Peacock Inn if you are not careful.

You speak also of Proust. The only really interesting thing about
Proust that I have seen recently is something that concerned him
as a poet. It seems like a revelation, but it is quite possible to say
that that is exactly what he was and perhaps all that he was. He
saw life on many levels, but what he wrote was always on the poetic
level on which he and you and I live. You are wrong, by the way,
in thinking that I read a lot of poetry. I don't read a line. My state
of mind about poetry makes me very susceptible and that is a danger
in the sense that it would be so easy for me to pick up something
unconsciously. In order not to run that danger I don't read other
people's poetry at all. There seem to be very few people who read
poetry at the finger tips, so to speak. This may be a surprise to you
but I am afraid it is the truth. Most people read it listening for
echoes because the echoes are familiar to them. They wade through
it the way a boy wades through water, feeling with his toes for the
bottom: the echoes are the bottom. This is something that I have
learned to do from Yeats who was extremely persnickety about
being himself. It is not so much that it is a way of being oneself
as it is a way of defeating people who look only for echoes and
influences.

I thought of you at Christmas time. Years ago when I was in
Cambridge I decided to stay up there on Christmas because it was
a pretty long trip to go home to Pennsylvania. Besides, I wanted to
attend one of the receptions which Charles Eliot Norton used to
give every Christmas to students who remained in Cambridge. It
was a forlorn experience. When the time came to go to the recep-
tion I said to myself the hell with it and spent the time sitting by
the fire. Cambridge on a holiday is like downtown New York on a
Sunday, but then there was nothing to do about it because when
one is feeling lonely nothing is better calculated to turn that mild
sadness into something bitter than sympathy.

It is nice to know that you regard all this weather as delightful.
This must be because it is good for the liver. Actually it is snowing
right now. I had never thought before that all of these white flakes
falling through the air were just so many little liver pills. What a

lot of medicine is going to flow down the Connecticut Valley when the sun, finally bored of its long winter in Cuba, comes up here to find out what life is really like.

With best wishes always,
Wallace Stevens

Ay, ay. Princeton, N?J?
At the Peacock Inn.
[January 1948]

Dear friend:

I came home to find your letter waiting here warm and cheerful. I left N.Y. in the middle of a blizzard, horrified at the probability of remaining imprisoned here for four weeks, buried in a small, trap-like hotel room, with only the grey, sick looking sky for companion. Indeed, it seems that those little white pills, the hell with the liver, are going to be the death of me, but I must confess a sort of sadistic pleasure at seeing myself enshrouded in all this whiteness and iciness. No wonder the liver responds livelier; after all in this frigid environment life assumes a sort of half-dormant condition, it does not grow old, but then one misses the sensual simmerings of southern shores and the regrets at those slow solar ascensions. By the way, I literally simper on those rare occasions when you choose to raise the little aspersorium (I hope I got it right in *English*) of your *ironía* over this your humble amigo. Witness that last phrase in your last letter when you speak of the sun coming north to see "what life is really like." Of course what is life really like here? Does it consummate itself in that busy rhythm which has afforded the visitors to your country's shores so many opportunities at the merry exercise, at the fair of the dénouement. See, if you want to be amused and at the same time a little saddened, the recent observations on the American scenery by Mr. Connolly in *Harpers*.[1] The only sense in scribbling those kinds of notes is to justify some people's retrenchment from life, even in a third floor pension. Which reminds me of the pleasure and the usufruct which dear old Henry

1. Cyril Connolly described the American "way" as "forty years' drudgery in an office." "Blue Print for a Silver Age: Notes on a Visit to America," *Harper's Magazine* (December 1947): 537–44.

made of the unfortunate fact that some bachelors will eventually end up in some pensions. I don't know if I, a born spectator in a fashion, will assemble all the bits and ends which one sometimes perceives scattered in those strange communities and weave a similarly odd figure—in the carpet, ever. The American pensions would, unless one violates the rigid limits of their imagination, encumber the possible way out—the creation of a *Daisy Miller,* where the heroine would be an American girl, not now doomed to frustration and death by a series of exotic motivations, but *rather* saved *for* life by the aseptic milieu into which she was fortunate to be born and reared. But you see the result would measure up to the popular tradition of the best sellers, unless . . . one does violation to the rigid and present the story in a less felicitous and happy light. Then, to cope with the material one needs indeed great gifts and maybe James went to Europe after all only because he knew (and he was a smart apple) that there his limited imagination could bring forth that rarer kind of flower, and only there. I can go on like this.

In N.Y. I went to see Bracque's show once more. The last time I went with Mariano, and we got into such exulted moods, with the barbarous exclamations and colorful gesturings which usually go with that kind of Latin mood, that sweet old Rosenberg came running out to ask us to be more sophisticated. I couldn't very well be that: not in a tête-a-tête with Mariano, who feels a passion for his art and worships Bracque. We went on, and Rosenberg finally left us with that quizzical look of the veteran who sees in all these impromptums the outbursts of earnest young men who feel but cannot afford to see the object of their feelings hanging in their poor little rooms. I was to meet Mr. Spender in town but the weather impeded us from carrying out the plan. He was to come from Scarsdale where he lives and rests from his laborious classes at Sarah Lawrence and I was to run up from Princeton where I avoid the labours of lectures and devise means to keep myself amused even when in the middle of a translation from a German text like Fieder Onkel and Diener Haus, which I found couldn't be transposed into my kind of lingo. Well, anyways we never met which I suppose was just as well since I was feeling very depressed.

You spoke in your letter about loneliness and how bitter our sadness turns upon seeing ourselves surrounded by people who are

trying to be sympathetic. It sounds very strange. I have lived a very
lonely life: my father died when I was very young, my mother was
ill then for a long time and I always remained away from home in
a boarding school. Later on, I went from one place to another,
always dwelt among strangers; and my few friends were dispersed
so that I could never see them again. Everything had gone to making my life rather lonely and sad; the anguish I feel must be explained by the fact that I was born to have friends and to feel with
an intensity not accorded to all the bonds of friendship, and yet I
do not have them and when I do find one, soon life sends him or
me away in opposite directions. Hence, sympathetic friends do not
embitter my days; rather they fill me with great joy and everlasting
gratitude. With all my loneliness, I thank God for those very few
friends I have had (two of the three I am thinking of are dead)
and look forward with certain confidence and hope to a future when
we shall meet again.

Please write soon. I liked the magazine you sent me and if you
have old copies around which you are intending to put into your
waste-paper basket, keep me in mind. I saw your Aurora poems.
What beautiful names you choose! I like them but won't enter into
a discussion lest I be labeled a shallow water swimmer, in search of
pretty echoes. I would like to know where you read about Proust,
le poète, unless you divined that yourself. I am reading *Causeries du
lundi* of Master Sainte-Beuve[2] and finding it very, very delicious
hors d'oeuvres before taking up the main dishes. You must admit
that sometimes his charming little resumés (of the works of Madame Du Deffand or the Abbé Galiani for example) leave us the
sensation of having tasted some delicate little morsel of fine food.

It is still snowing here but life has not yet caught up with me,
unfortunately.

Yours devotedly,
José

2. Charles-Augustin Sainte-Beuve, *Causeries du Lundi* (Paris: Garnier,
1853–62).

[Hartford, Connecticut]
February 17, 1948

Dear José:

Ça va bien. I have a number of copies of the Statesman at home which I shall drop in the mail sooner or later, but I have not yet finished reading them and at the moment have suspended all reading until I am able to dispose of something else. After I have walked home when I would ordinarily have a glass of water and a few cookies and sit down in an easy chair with the evening paper, I go upstairs nowadays and work over my chore like one of the holy fathers working over his prayers. In fact, this morning I was up at five o'clock under the impression that it was six and did not discover my mistake until I had finished my bath and was half-dressed, when it was too late to go back to bed. I thought that the darkness was due to the mist when in fact it was not due to anything: it was just dark.

I am writing merely to keep in touch with you.

Do you know La Licorne? Probably you can find the second number of it (Hiver 1947) which has just come out. It contains an extraordinarily touching souvenir of Bernard Groethuysen by Jean Paulhan.[1] I did not even know that Groethuysen was dead. He was something of a mystic, but he was a man of the widest interest in philosophy. The Paulhans and the Groethuysens seem to have had adjoining ateliers in Paris. Groethuysen was impractical to the extent that when the gas jet in his room began to sing he was frightened to death and ran next door to Paulhan's place to ask for help. I have offered to lend my copy of the thing to Mrs. Church so that I cannot send it to you.

Lebewohl. Dichtung und Wahrheit Über Alles!

Wallace Stevens

---

1. *La Licorne* 2 (Winter 1948) contains Paulhan's remembrance of Bernard Groethuysen. The section "Groeth dans son Atelier" charmingly recalls Groethuysen's habits, such as smoking herbal cigarettes and going about "en pyjama, en pantalon."

[Princeton, New Jersey]
February 18 [1948]

My dear friend:

Your letter came to brighten up a little my existence. Only a few hours before I had a call from Habana telling me of mother's illness. I have probably told you that she becomes ill every two or three years of a nervous ailment which requires her confinement in a sanatorium. Although she had been suffering this sickness since the age of 18, I have seen her many times go through that intermediate period when her mind's lucidity is clouded over and she begins to lose her hold on reality, I have never quite become used to it. It always comes as a shock. My brother, Orlando, took her to the sanatorium and after he closed the house, he took the boat to Miami. He's coming to N.Y. because his wife is having a baby next month. I expect to return home soon, although I cannot do anything for mother, but wait around until she recovers, I feel I should be there, nearby. Her illness lasts from 4 to 8 months so I don't know if I shall return to Princeton in time to enter the Graduate School. My friends say that I shouldn't sacrifice everything for her sake, that I must live *my* own life and not worry so much over her. It's all very well said, but I feel that one hour of her suffering is not made up by anything I or anyone else can do. Besides, there is nothing one can do, when it is the heart and not a sense of duty or piety that moves us to act this or that way.

I went to Philadelphia last Tuesday to hear Britten's opera, "Peter Grimes." It was wonderfully done although it requires great skill on the actor's and singer's part of the characters. It is a very powerful music, the sort of thing one gets used to not hearing nowadays.[1] I would like to hear it again; the first time one listens to new music the ear is pricked for analysis of themes and motives and one cannot relax enough to let the music just flow in and take hold of our soul.

I have not seen *La Licorne*. Princeton's library is rather insufficient in modern literature and reviews. I will look around in N.Y. for a copy for I would like to see Paulhan's article.

1. On Tuesday, 17 February, the Metropolitan Opera had presented the Philadelphia premiere of Benjamin Britten's opera, conducted by Emil Cooper. Frederick Jagel enacted the title role, with Regina Resnik and John Brownlee.

I have been reading a lot now. *Burr Oaks* of Richard Eberhart;[2] *The Beautiful Changes* of R[ichard] Wilbur;[3] and in prose E[dmund] Wilson's *Europe Without a Baedeker*,[4] and *Anna Karenina*. Wilson's book was superficial; hysterical in his observations of the English and Italians, and rather a bore considering the man's intellectual competence. One notices the subtle adaptation of *tone* and feeling to the *New Yorkish* cast of reader and wonders how such an intelligent critic could have ended in this rather foolish position. His interview with Santayana, in the book, is a good example of what I mean. You must get the book if only for this brief view of the old man.

Have you seen [Sacheverell] Sitwell's *The Hunter and the Hunted* (!)?[5] Someone spoke of the book the other day with great enthusiasm. So I will have to find out if it's so good. I hope to go to N.Y. soon. If you are planning a trip, let me know and I will try to make our trips coincide.

Now it's very warm. The snow is melting and last Sunday I saw a cardinal (the bird) chirping about the oak tree outside my window. There was a bluejay, too, but he did not surprise me so much as this note of red with the white background.

Please write soon. And do let me know if you are going to New York soon.

Yours devotedly,
José R. Feo

[Havana]
March 13 [1948]

My dear poet:

I do not envy you today. I have just seen in the papers that another cold wave has covered the East with snow. And I am here. The sun shines, there is a marvelous tropical breeze floating thru the

2. New York: Oxford University Press, 1947.
3. New York: Reynal and Hitchcock, 1947.
4. Edmund Wilson, *Europe Without Baedeker: Sketches among the Ruins of Italy, Greece and England* (Garden City, N.Y.: Doubleday, 1947).
5. London: Macmillan, 1947.

mangos, and cocoteros. In the evenings it is very delightful; I usually go for a stroll after spending the afternoon reading Spanish lit. In the morning I study my German.

Mother is ill with her usual nervous crisis, but this time it is not too bad. So I hope soon she will be back, because it is very lonely indeed to stay in this big empty house all by myself.

I have just read *The Loved One* by Evelyn Waugh, a novelette which takes up a whole issue of *Horizon*[1] and pictures the inadequacies of the Californian sense of death. It is amazing Connolly[2] should present this story as one of the best in modern times. It is actually "lousy"; I cannot find another word to tell you how horrible it is. After you have finished it, you seem to remember nothing but the irate and confused propaganda of another Britisher who has roamed around the States just to be able to say some smart and clever things about American civilization. There is nothing original or profound in his observations just as Connolly's article on America was a conglomeration of the cliches and common places you have been hearing since Tocqueville came ashore. But as I have always said: the English are never so disdainful as when in defeat. All that talk about fair play is just another formula they put forward to justify their inherent weakness. Because it seems to me that with all their shrewdness and common sense, the English are essentially a stupid race. Of course, that doesn't prevent them from giving us some of the greatest geniuses of all times. And it seems significant that their greatest man is Shakespeare, a dramatist. And their longest and most honourable institution is the lyric poetry in which they have been so magnificent. Last night, I was talking to [Harold?] Osborne, an English painter who has lived most of his life outside of England, five years here in Matanzas and the rest of the time travelling about. He said that the horrible thing about Englishmen is that they spent their lives learning wisdom and other things from "experience" and then they come into relation with the Spaniards and find a common, everyday uneducated Spaniard who has all that he has per se and *more,* that more means that they actually *live* all that possession. He added rather pathetically that he would wish

1. *Horizon* 17, no. 98 (February 1948).
2. The editor of *Horizon,* Cyril Connolly.

he had been born a Spaniard. Can you imagine an Englishman of
the 16th or 17th centuries making that confession?

Yesterday I went down to the ocean and dipped in. It was wonderful, the water was transparent blue-green and warm compared
to that cold stream in which I used to bathe in Vermont in August.
Of course, the natives do not go swimming. It is too damn cold for
them just now. By the way, have read Camus' *La Peste*. I believe it
is the most important novel since *The Magic Mountain*. In Mann's
book the allegory takes place in a rarified atmosphere where a
crystal cold makes his creatures look embalmed; here the action
takes place in North Africa and it is another allegory of our times
but more powerful and human and less intellectual, that is to say
less german-philosophical. I have had one of the sections from this
book, *Noces,* translated for *Orígenes*.[3]

I hope the weather does not get you down and you will have time
to pen me a few lines. I wish you a Merry Eastern with bunnies and
golden Eggs and all that. I am as ever your admiring Caribe,

Pepe

[A handwritten note from Stevens has not been found.]

[Havana]
April 9 [1948]

My Dear Walacio:

Your letter came inscribed in beautiful but cryptic signs. Perhaps,
I am becoming rather too easy going under this splendent tropical
light; I find all things become more difficult to decipher: life as well
as literature. My wish is that your luxurious and lucky secretary will
be soon again at 690 Asylum to note down all your thoughts in that
horrible but more lucid Remingtonese language that H. James also
found so much more convenient an instrument.

Uh, it must be wonderful to see the green grass shyly showing
its new blades and the flowers making an effort, what an effort up

3. An excerpt from *The Plague* appeared in the spring 1948 issue (vol.
5, no. 17, pp. 23–27).

there in Connecticut all those simple natural things have to make, to bloom again. Here the sea is the perennial wonder to these my eyes; I never tire of alleging to my blind friends that all Cubans live with their backs turned to the sea which is a strange phenomenon which makes us not islanders at all and create in their minds the peculiar sensation of having been banished from some paradise. I believe that same paradise is the lovely blue, green mauve sea which all around encircles us. It comes to my mind that Cuba instead of depending on Sugar and tobacco should have derived her wealth from the sea. Just like other island-states. But that is another of the anomalies which you will discover if you were to reside here for a little while.

Mother is getting well very rapidly this time and I think soon she will be home again. I am now at another crossroad: must decide whether I shall return to Princeton or get a job and stay here. You see, if I go, she will be alone here again. For my brother Orlando Furioso is married now and will not return to live with her: the reason is that his wife (an American) does not like the idea. Independence and all that. Oh America! Speaking of painting: I saw the Mexican show here. I finally came to the conclusion (suspected it a long time however) that Rivera, Orozco and Siqueiros are all terribly overrated and are really now embarked upon an academic stage which reveals their decadence. The Cubans are less pretentious, more charming and some have produced works which surpassed the bloody, screaming, cultural and nationalistic propaganda of the mejicanos.[1]

I was very happy, Walacio, to get your letter. You were very silent for a long time. I accept your excuse. If you have an extra copy of the *Hudson Review* which presents your new poems, will you send me a copy?[2] And whenever you have any English or French magazine that you do not want, send them to me. Soon I shall send you *Orígenes* and *The Anthology of Cuban Poets* (1937–1947) which is in the press now.

1. The Mexican painters José Clemente Orozco and David Alfaro Siqueiros together led a renaissance of mural painting in the 1920s. With Diego Rivera, they were well known by this time for their large public works; see José's letter of 19 December 1946.
2. "In a Bad Time," *Hudson Review* 1 (Spring 1948): 29.

I am not very happy here. Nowhere. But I sleep my siesta, go for
a walk in the evening with the sea breeze for a companion and read
and write a little. That is all and I am contented. I have a strange
feeling I will not live very long. I am just waiting for mother, because I *know* she could never in her delicate mind bear the loss of
her son.

Yours affectionately as ever,
José

[Hartford, Connecticut]
May 4, 1948

Dear José

When I was in New York not long ago I dropped in to see
Mariano's pictures. I hope that he is not all out of breath waiting to
know whether I like them because the truth is that I didn't. I
thought that they were lurid and rhetorical.

As you know, I pay just as much attention to painters as I do to
writers because, except technically, their problems are the same.
They seem to move in the same direction at the same time. You and
I know that when a poet is writing merely like other poets it
amounts to this: that when he is in New York he writes like the
poets in New York, but if he moves to Paris, he writes like the
poets in Paris. The same thing is true of painters. I just don't think
that Mariano is being himself. Since I believe in him, the only thing
to do is to wait until he really becomes himself.

I think that all this abstract painting that is going on nowadays
is just so much frustration and evasion. Eventually it will lead to a
new reality. When a thing has been blurred by the obscurity of
metaphysics and eventually emerges from that blur, it has all the
characteristics of a brilliantly clear day after a month of mist and
rain. No-one can predict what that new reality is going to be because it will be developed in the mind and spirit and by the hand
of a single artist or group of artists strong enough to conceive of
what they want and to produce it. I am saying that particularly with
reference to painting. It is certainly no less true with reference to
poetry and even to politics.

Feigl[1] seems to think very well of Mariano and he told me that he was having considerable success. There is not the slightest doubt that Mariano is an interesting figure. But a man does not achieve himself by willing to do something: he does it as part of the experience of himself: of living his own life in his own world. I don't believe that his pictures in his last show are a true part of Mariano's experience of himself.

I didn't want to reply to your last letter until I was able to say something about Mariano that was both just and simple. I leave it to you whether to tell him that I was not able to get down to New York and therefore could not see his show or whether to tell him what I have just said. One of these days when you are both up here together we must arrange to meet.

One thing that the individual painter develops is his individual doctrine. In part, what you disliked in Mexican paintings seems to have been the generalized doctrine of Mexican painting. Somehow Mexican painting seems to undertake to teach. This makes it academic in spirit even when it is not academic in manner, or so it seems. God forbid that I should discourse on Mexican painting, about which I know so little, or for that matter, on any painting.

If things go well this summer, I hope to accomplish more or less. During the last several months I have been busy clearing up a tremendous accumulation at home of things to read. Now at last I have reached a point at which when I go home in the evening there is nothing for me to do after I have read the Hartford Times and have had a glass of orange juice except to enjoy life: to try and get the feel of it and to think about it and to work on it. This is an intense pleasure but it requires almost total leisure. I have promised a good many poems to people. These come very easy or not at all and I hope soon, with this new freedom and wider margin, to reach a point at which I may be able to do enough to send something to everyone. Are you writing? I had thought that in the absence of anything from Germany and with the dilution of interest that everyone must feel in what is coming to us from France and again in the absence of anything, or almost anything, from England I was going

1. Hugo Feigl (1890–1961), Czech art dealer and founder of his Madison Avenue gallery in 1942, specialized in French and German Expressionist painting.

to have an opportunity to think about many things that had origi-
nated in one or the other of those places. But, suddenly, I began to
think about Switzerland. There is a great deal coming from Switzerland. Then, too, Switzerland is something that one ought to think
about in the summertime. It is so much more agreeable to think
about Lake Geneva at this time of year than it is to think about the
rue de Babylone, nicht wahr?

> Adios,
> Wallace Stevens

> La Habana
> June 3 [1948]

My dear Mr. Stevens:

Just a few lines to let you know that I received your nice, long
letter. I haven't written because I underwent an operation last week.
It was an ulcer in the rectum which affected a hemorrhoid. The doctor was very worried because he feared it might be of tubercular or
cancerous origin. But it was not so malignant. The doctor is a graduate of the Mayo clinic. Very fine. A young fellow. The operation
didn't hurt but the wound is very sensitive and it takes a long time
to close up.

I am destined therefore to spend a summer in bed, although I
shall probably be up in a month and will go to Varadero with
mother.

I am sorry I have only these rather vulgar notices to offer. When
I feel better I shall write. Meantimes, do let me know of yourself. I
am as ever,

> José

> [Hartford, Connecticut]
> June 14, 1948

Dear José

I am sorry to hear of your trouble. The truth is that I rather
thought that you or your mother might be ill.

It has been prodigiously dull up here. The almost continual rain
has been bad enough, but it has been cold and gray or hot and gray

or just gray. And I have not been able to get away from it by flying
to Switzerland, say, or by attending King Michael's wedding.[1] In
recent years it has meant at least a little something to me to go to
New York for a day: to buy a raincoat, to choose wall paper, to
look at books from Europe, to walk through the streets. But all this
bad weather has brought it about that I say that I already have a
raincoat, that the present wall paper is good enough, that it is hope-
less to get anywhere by reading, that the streets are all dug up anyway and, in general, the hell with it.

Perhaps I am beginning to think permanently, and without regard to the weather, that one gets nowhere by reading. Nowadays it
is common-place to speak of the role of the writer in the world of
today. But why not think and speak of the role of the reader of
Orígenes, the role of the reader of my poetry, say, in the midst
of the contemporary conspiracy and in the midst of the contemporary conspirators. Would not one's time be better spent seated in an
excellent restaurant on the shore of Lac de Genève (Genfersee to
students of German) listening to a sacred concert of a beautiful
Sunday evening and meditating? Is not a meditation after soup of
more consequence than reading a chapter of a novel before dinner?
We do not spend enough time in thought and again when we think
we usually do it on an empty stomach. I cannot believe that the
world would not be a better world if we reflected on it after a really
advantageous dinner. How much misery the aphorisms of empty
people have caused!

Well, however that may be, I have a new correspondent, a citizen
of Dublin, a fellow of great piety but otherwise of impeccable taste.
It seems that troupes of singers of operas fly from Paris to Dublin,
fill the night air with Mélisande, then go to a party and fly back to
Paris, all in a single circuit of the clock. What a dazzling diversion.
And I am sure that even without such things one is never bored in
Dublin because with all the saints they know, and know of, there,
there is always company of a kind and in Dublin saints are the best

1. The complications of King Michael's wedding would have been making big news. Formerly the king of Rumania, whose abdication was believed to have been forced by the Communists, Michael was living in exile
in Switzerland. His elaborate wedding to Princess Ann of Bourbon took
place four days before this letter was written.

company in the world.[2] There are no saints at all in Hartford. Very
likely they exist at Varadero Beach, walking by the turquoise water
and putting ideas into one's head, with nothing to do except to
water the geraniums on the window sill (and, I hope, write an occasional letter to Hartford). All the time one would be finding out
about life. It would come to one without trouble like a revelation
and it would ripen and take on color. I am speaking of Lebens-
weisheit, which is what one particularly picks up on beaches and in
the presence of one-piece bathing suits.

We have on a table in the dining room several Hayden mangoes.
What healthy looking things they are. A friend who has been to
Munich wrote to me the other day of the extent of the destruction
of "blue and white Munich." It is like changing records on a gramophone to speak of the red and the almost artificial green of mango
skins and then speak of blue and white Munich.[3] But unless we do
these things to reality, the damned thing closes us in,[4] walls us up
and buries us alive. After all, as you spend your summer getting
well again, aren't you in an extraordinary position to carry on the
struggle with and against reality and against the fifth column of
reality that keeps whispering with the hard superiority of the sane
that reality is all we have, that it is that or nothing. Reality is the

2. The new correspondent was Thomas McGreevy, the Irish Catholic
poet. In May McGreevy had sent Stevens copies of two of his books. In
seven years of letters, McGreevy created for the Hartford poet a Dublin
to match José's Havana—luscious and full of familiar saints. Stevens tolerated the Irishman's "habit of almost medieval faith"; "I like the God
bless you with which he winds up his letters," he wrote (L, 682).
3. The phrase "blue and white Munich" is taken from a note he received from Barbara Church, the widow of Henry Church. When he used
the phrase three months later at Columbia University in his lecture
"Imagination as Value," the relations between Barbara Church's Munich,
Thomas McGreevy's Dublin, and José's Havana had shifted, but his point
was the same: "It is a commonplace to realize the extent of artifice in the
external world and to say that Florence is more imaginative than Dublin,
that blue and white Munich is more imaginative than white and green
Havana, and so on. . . . What is engaging us at the moment has nothing
to do with the external world. We are concerned with the question of its
value." NA, 140–41.
4. We have emended Stevens' "closes in us" to "closes us in," thereby
maintaining a parallelism he must have intended.

footing from which we leap after what we do not have and on which everything depends. It is nice to be able to think of José combatting the actual in Cuba, grasping great masses of it and making out of those masses a gayety of the mind.

What makes life difficult here or anywhere else is not the material of which it is made but the failure to use it. I could argue that against all the rabbis in the world. But then the rabbis would not argue against it. The things that we build or grow to do are so little when compared to the things that we suggest or believe or desire.

Sincerely yours,
Wallace Stevens

La Habana
June 19 [1948]

My dear visionary:

Everybody was ill around here. Now I am much better, and mother will be coming home next week. So this morning I am going to town wearing my pink shirt, the scandalous shirt which the family always take as a definitive detail of my good, jolly recovery. Mother is the only person who consents: she figures that I might be starting a mode and that I have as good a reason for wearing pink as for blue or grey. She is very sensible; a remarkable woman, although she has never read a book since she left school (a nunnery in Pou) and retains more wisdom than all I have been able to squeeze out of a few books and disconcerting experiences. Once I mentioned Stalin in a conversation with some good Communists who happened to go in for culture too, and she asked me if he had married Chencha, a mulatto girl who lives nearby. I was stupidly taken in and my two friends (the Reds) gave her a dirty look. Then I realized that she had misunderstood me and thought I had said Balin, a chofer (white) who had been running after Chencha for a long time. But it was too late. My friends left in disgust and I had to give mother a lesson in modern history to avoid further complications. But in the end she was bored with the whole story and told me I was making up the whole thing. So next day I had her read the paper, just one paragraph where the name Stalin is mentioned rather ungraciously by some American correspondent. But when she asked why they called him certain names, I had to give up. Still she knows more about cows, horses and chickens than most people I know, who read Plato and Proust; she wanted to name her newly-born colt Platon but I told her the name was too precious and she said that it was musical and went well with his languid eyes. Imagine that. You cannot mention strange, exotic names in front of her; one never knows where they are going to pop up again.

I am hoping to go to Varadero soon. I think your vision of the dear place is most touching. I suggest you visit us and avoid the grey skies of Hartford. One here gets fed up with blue skies, and golden, violet sunsets. I would like to have an Anglo-Saxon about to dis- cover or re-discover our wonders.

We have moved to a new apartment near the sea. Our old house is being fixed. So I have the benefit of a nice cool sea breeze. I sit in the terrace (we live in a third floor) and read [Oscar] Milosz's *L'amoureuse Initiation*.[1] It is a strange novel like everything this Lithuanian wrote. His poems are sort of Balkan Rilkean. I finished [Italo] Svevo's *Confessions of Zeno*.[2] But I will leave him for an- other day. I must go now to see my tailor. I am wearing the amazing tie you gave me in New York so that you can imagine the blaze of colors I walk in.

> Yours devotedly,
> José

[Stevens received this letter mailed from Havana only two days after it was written, on Monday the twenty-first. He immediately summarized the letter for Barbara Church and commented: "How much more this mother knows than her son who reads Milosz and Svévò. She is controlled by the force that attaches; he by the force that detaches; and both are puppets on the strings of their relation- ship to reality. She shrinks from leaving home; he, from remaining there." And, he added, "The Stevenses shrink from everything" (*L*, 602).]

1. The collected works of Milosz had begun to be published in 1944 (Fribourg: Egloff).
2. Translated by Beryl de Zoete (New York: Knopf, 1930).

[Havana]
July 30 [1948]

Mon cher poète:

Habana is very French now. Last night I saw Henri de Monther-lant's "Le Maitre Santiago,"[1] the wonderful historic drama about the Master of the Order of Santiago who refused to have anything in the Imperial policy of Spain. His idea was this: Spain after the conquest of Granada went haywire; she should have turned inward, into her soul, and not have gone after vain, perishable glories in the New World. It is acted out with great conviction. There was a Franco's gentleman, from the Spanish Embassy, behind me in the theater and he said: "The idea is absurd." Of course, it is. Where would I be otherwise? But you see Henri is discovering now (Paris is always behind in these matters) the old theories of Ganivet, and the whole Spanish generation of 1898 who came out against de-generation of the Spanish energies in exterior enterprises and who blamed the Empire for all the evils which fell on the Spanish nation. Thus, you see Unamuno crying out for the *Españiolizacion de Europa,*[2] the Spanishation of Europe (how would you pronounce the second word?) Of course, the absurd point here is to discuss and argue about "what could have been if," and to forget what they have, now. The French company is going to give our public the benefit of Existentialism. They are doing *Huis-Clos* of Sartre and later *Mede,* the modern version of Jean Anouilh. Later on we shall be happy to see "Monsieur Lamberthier" de [Louis] Verneuil. The actors are Ivonne Scheffer and Rene Rolland of the Comedie Fran-çais. The French pictures are back: the delightful Cocteau's *La Belle et la Bête,* Radiguet's *Le Diable au Corps* and the last Che-valier film.[3]

1. Henri de Montherlant (1896–1972) was a French novelist, essayist, and dramatist, whose early works exalted war, sports, bullfighting, and the cult of the body.
2. See, for example, Miguel de Unamuno y Jugo, *Avant et Après la Revolution,* trans. Jean Cassou (Paris: Rieder, 1933), which includes such essays as "Espagne, Espagne, Espagne."
3. Both Jean Cocteau's version of "Beauty and the Beast" and the film based on Raymond Radiguet's 1925 novel, directed by Claude Autant-Lara, had been released in 1946. Maurice Chevalier's recent picture was *Paris 1900* (1948).

Speaking of England, now we have the Olympic games. I would prefer frankly to see a regatta on the Henley or a Track meet than some of the horrible cultural activities we have to suffer here. Sometimes I think about it all and would have preferred to have been a great athlete than an "intelligent youth." Take my friend Patricio. He has a beautiful build and the most amazing green eyes. Just to look at him you tremble with fascination. Result: all the pretty girls at the Yacht Club gather around in stupid admiration. To see Patricio you would think he has the most wonderful things to say. But yesterday he talked for a whole hour about the last victories of the Red Sox and the comeback of Zulueta, a Cuban boxer.

Where am I? Here in Habana. I haven't been able to get away. That old hack Bacon, who used to say that man is never so lonely as in the city, was right. He also was most pragmatic and used to enumerate the fruits of friendship like boxes of candy to be sent to this or that lady. In his essay on Happiness[4] (or is there such an essay?), he never mentions that state of being which I have come to consider more terrible than either happiness or unhappiness, where one is neither of the two. It is hard to describe, but I think more people share it than are willing to admit it. For instance, yesterday I bought some peaches. I wanted to try out the Proustian trick and get some remembrances of things past in Vermont. It failed. The peaches were sour. Then I knew that state I speak of, above: the peaches had failed me; Proust was a liar. Maybe that is the difference in existing in a realm of art or in a realm of sour peaches.

I told mother about your theories of names, in reference to Platon, her cow. She thinks you are a very sensible person and asked me if you too kept a cow and a few chickens in far away Hartford. I said you certainly did. Otherwise, you would have suffered a sharp dip in her estimation. But perhaps you do.

---

4. The essay by Bacon to which José refers is "On Friendship." He was remembering this passage: "For a crowd is not company, and faces are but a gallery of pictures, and talk but a tinkling cymbal, where there is no love. The Latin adage meeteth with it a little, Magna civitas, magna solitudo; because in a great town friends are scattered; so that there is not the fellowship for the most part, which is in less neighbourhoods."

Every afternoon it rains like hell here. It is a pleasant Invitation
to a Siesta. So I must close feeling I have given you a tip for a wonderful poem. By the way, has "The Owl in the Sarcophagus" appeared in print, in book form? I wanted to translate it. I have lost
my copy of the *Horizon* in which it appeared originally.[5] Another
thing. [William] Van [O']Connor in his essay on Mr. Stevens
mentions two essays which I don't have a name? Where are they
published?[6]

Hasta pronto.
José

[Princeton, New Jersey]
Sept. 21 [1948]

My dear Mr. Stevens:

I have been in Princeton three days and already I feel like an old
professor, accustomed to rushing to classrooms, harping on the
need of a new textbook, disgusted with the meals and the other
teachers' conversations. You see I am here teaching Spanish composition; I study Spanish lit. at the same time, in preparation for
my Ph.D. Soon I will be taking the French reading Exam. I have
settled down, in a gloomy room off the Campus to prepare myself
for an academic life. I gave up a job [offer] at the Unesco at Paris
because mother was afraid I would freeze in the Parisian hotels. She
happened to listen in on a conversation wherein a friend of mine
described in gruesome details the fate of an Argentine writer. At
night he would go to bed, cover himself with blankets—protruding
from the pile of wool a hand, in a black glove, holds a novel by
Camus. That was the only safe way he could keep in touch with
French literary events. Mother was much impressed by the picture
of the engloved hand holding a trembling little volume. She begged
me to stay away. To come to Princeton seemed safer. So here I am.

Dear old Nassau won't be so dull after all. T. S. Eliot will be here

5. "The Owl in the Sarcophagus" first appeared in *Horizon* 93–94
(October 1947): 58–62. It was never published as a separate pamphlet but
appeared in *The Auroras of Autumn* (1950).
6. William Van O'Connor mentions only "The Figure of the Youth as
Virile Poet," *Sewanee Review* 52, no. 4 (Fall 1944): 508–29.

soon[1] and J[acques] Maritain will be lecturing on Thomism (?).
But I miss already Cuba's warmth and its blue and gold. I even feel
a certain nostalgia when I read that another hurricane has come
blowing through the Isle. I would have liked to be in the middle of
"things."

My long silence must be blamed on the American foreign service
which kept me for weeks rushing about. I had a terrible time before
I could get that precious resident visa. Now I can stay here forever,
"as long as you behave" as the nice Irish Immigration officer put it.

I hope you had a nice summer. I remembered you often in Varadero; I wonder what it would have been like had you escaped from
H. and landed in that lovely Caribbean beach. For instance, its effect
on your poetry. ¡Cuántas nuevas tonalidades, verdes, azules, oros!
Qué alegria![2] By the way, have you published any new poems
lately? Will you be coming to Princeton this year? I hope you do.
We must see each other soon. I have many things to talk over with
you. If I might be so fresh as to expect your interest in my modest
life. Have you read Jean Cassou's *Panorama de la Littérature Es-
pagnole Contemporaine?*[3] It has a wonderful essay on Spain and
the Spaniard called "L'Espange: Valeur Spirituelle." Do look it up.
I enjoyed very much your little essay on M[arianne] Moore, which
seems a beautiful *retrato* of her own queer style.[4] Her own poems
in the *Quarterly Review of Literature*[5] I found a bit of a disappointment. I don't know why.

Will you write soon? I am very busy but I will find a moment
to write you again and let you know how things are coming along.
You know I am always anxious to hear from you.

Saludos cordiales,

José

1. Eliot had been invited to become a visiting fellow at the Institute for
Advanced Studies at Princeton and embarked for America in late September. Peter Ackroyd, *T. S. Eliot: A Life* (New York: Simon and Schuster,
1984), 287.
2. "How many new tonalities, greens, blues, golds! What joy!"
3. Paris: Éditions Kra, 1931.
4. "About One of Miss Moore's Poems," *Quarterly Review of Literature* 4 (Summer 1948): 143–49, was included in *NA*, 93–103.
5. "By Disposition of Angels," "La Fontaine Precepts," and "Voracities
and Verities."

[Hartford, Connecticut]
October 6, 1948

Dear José:

You failed to give me your address in the letter that you wrote me a couple of weeks ago, but, with the help of the F.B.I., I have found that you are living at 2 Dickinson Street, Princeton.

I mean to write you a real letter before long. What I want to do now is ask whether you have any objection to my publishing the poem[1] a copy of which you will find enclosed. This in no way identifies you but the language is verbatim from your letter.

Sincerely yours,
Wallace Stevens

[Princeton, New Jersey]
[Oct. 8, 1948]

My dear Spaniard:

What a charming idea to set to music and lovely poetry (bella poesía) my discursive meditation on a homely theme! ¡Qué honor, Dios mio! I really feel almost like blushing.

You do have my permission to print it. What objection could I have to poetry?

I shall write you soon and tell you about mother's latest whims and pleasures. It will amuse you as it has moved me deeply. But I must close now, as I am going to Philadelphia to see a Quaker amigo and to hear a bit of Music.

Eliot is around but so well disguised that I cannot detect him. I hope to see him soon. I am anxious to feel his pulse. Does it beat still with the same "primaveral" gusto that shines through your adivinations. What else is "The Novel" but an adivination of what could have happened if only the man had taken to *live* his black, enshrouded moment. I feel that we all nowadays abhor *la tristeza* and feel that a shot at Xavier Cougat or a game of basketball will cure us of all our predicaments. And perhaps that explains our lack of gusto. And the final monotony and sadness of our faces as we go up the hill can be explained by our fear of tears.

1. "The Novel."

Finally, I would like to know how you hit upon my address. It could be a compliment or a sinister issue of the persecution of the minorities!

Yours in gratitude and alegría,
José

[Hartford, Connecticut]
October 25, 1948

Dear José:

The poem will be published eventually in Philadelphia by a printer there with illustrations of some sort. John Alden, the curator of rare books in the University of Pennsylvania library asked for it. Since you failed to send me your address, I supposed that he would have some friend in the library at Princeton who could track you down, and so it turned out. I shall send you a copy when it appears. The time is indefinite.[1]

At the moment I feel completely illiterate, so to speak. I rather think that nature gets at me more thoroughly now than at any other time of the year. One grows used to spring; and summer and winter become bores. But Otonno! How this oozing away hurts notwithstanding the pumpkins and the glaciale of frost and the onslaught of books and pictures and music and people. It is finished, Zarathustra says; and one goes to the Canoe Club and has a couple of Martinis and a pork chop and looks down the spaces of the river and participates in the disintegration, the decomposition, the rapt finale. Murder . . . and adieu; assassination . . . and farewell.

And, somehow, for all the newness in this world in which every

1. Stevens had sent "The Novel" to John Alden on 28 September. It was to be printed, with illustrations, by a friend with a private press. "José is José Rodríguez-Feo of Havana," Stevens wrote Alden. "He wrote to me from Princeton a few weeks ago and the language quoted is taken from his letter. . . . I suppose that as a matter of decency I ought to let him know that I am using this although there is nothing to identify him in its use because there are as many José's as there are Johns." See *L,* 617n, n. 6. In February 1950, when Stevens gathered poems for the manuscript of *The Auroras of Autumn,* Alden's friend still had not printed "The Novel"; Stevens wrote Alden again and withdrew the poem. Stevens to Alden, 9 February 1950, Van Pelt Library, University of Pennsylvania.

familiar thing is being replaced by something unfamiliar, in which
all the weak affect to be strong, and all the strong keep silence, one
has a sense that the world was never less new than now, never more
an affair of routine, never more mechanical and lacking in any
potency of fineness. Nicht wahr? It is as if modern art, modern
letters, modern politics had at last demonstrated that they were
merely diversions, merely things to be abandoned when the time
came to pick up the ancient burden again and carry it on. What I
mean is getting rid of all our horrid fiction and getting back to the
realities of mankind. Perhaps instead of living in an era of man
released at last from history, we are living in a period of a lot of
damned nonsense. I cannot help feeling that communism, in spite
of its organization, in spite of its revolutionary program and detona-
tions, is the bunk: something specious, the refuge of failure.

I am writing, as you detect, in the mood of autumn, the mood in
which one sums up and meditates on the actualities of the actual
year. What has this late year meant to me as a reasonably intelligent
and reasonably imaginative person? What music have I heard that
has not been the music of an orchestra of parrots and what books
have I read that were not written for money and how many men of
ardent spirit and star-scimitar mind have I met? Not a goddam one.
And I think it is because the world in general is not really moving
forward. There is no music because the only music tolerated is modern music. There is no painting because the only painting permitted
is painting derived from Picasso or Matisse. And of course there are
very few living individuals because we are all compelled to live in
clusters: unions, classes, the West, etc. Only in such pious breasts
as yours and mine does freedom still dwell. When I go into a fruit
store nowadays and find there nothing but the fruits du jour: apples,
pears, oranges, I feel like throwing them at the Greek. I expect, and
you expect, sapodillas and South Shore bananas and pineapples a
foot high with spines fit to stick in the helmet of a wild chieftain.

You probably asked me a lot of questions in your last letter. I
ignore them. Why should I answer questions from young philoso-
phers when I receive perfumed notes from Paris? What I really like
to have from you is not your tears on the death of Bernanos, say,
but news about chickens raised on red peppers and homesick rhapsodies of the Sienese look of faraway Havana and news about people

I don't know, who are more fascinating to me than all the characters in all the novels of Spain, which I am unable to read.

Cordial salutes,
Wallace Stevens

[Princeton, New Jersey]
Nov. 15 [1948]

My dear friend:

Sorry to have been so long in answering. Work and classes have kept me far too busy!

The climate is lovely here! Mother writes that it is very warm in Habana, the blue flamboyant looks like a chandelier with its piles of blue petals. She says that the grandchildren are well. The little girl (6 months) she calls "cucaracha," I don't know why! and "little log of wood," because she's fat and red and "little worm" because she gets out from under the covers like a worm. Imagine!

I haven't seen Mr. Eliot yet. Now that he is A nobel, it's harder because he hides from reporters.[1] I saw him from afar in Oppenheimer's lecture on his trip to Europe. I told Mr. Blackmur the story of the man in Paris and he was much impressed and keeps telling everyone. I don't see him often. Too busy too. Why are all Americans so busy nowadays?

I have been reading Emerson for a report to the American Lit. Seminar. He's a marvelous man. I was surprised to see him use words like "agate," "give me agates for meat," and "sherbet" and "parakeet" [?] in a way which reminded me of your poems and he has a poem which seems written by M. Moore. An extraordinary man!

I hope you will be having time to go to N.Y. soon—I am planning to go some Saturday. Can we arrange to meet? I am free Saturday and Sunday. Maybe you can arrange it. I would like to talk to you. I have so many things to tell you about which in print seem inadequate.

I am quite happy now. Working and reading and teaching have

1. Eliot received official word that he had won the Nobel Prize for Literature in November. By the end of the month he left Princeton for London and Stockholm. Ackroyd, *T. S. Eliot,* 289.

brought me some peace of mind. Or let's say that it has closed a
door on many thoughts which in a state of leisure assail and make
me unhappy. But I wonder if it's really an advantage. It makes for
sedentary life, emotionally I mean. It has the tendency of making us
a bit of an automat, intellectual, and to make us forget the passionate side of life. How can we cultivate the passions in Princeton.
They dry up here and we float through the campus, classes and
Firestone library a disembodied body, pure spirit, in the air like a
gas-balloon.

Last night I had a furious argument. Mr. King was complaining
about someone's lack of nicety and sincerity. So I told him, "I don't
care for niceness, the hell with sincerity. Let's be insincere" and he
got angry and called me an immoral Cuban. I really meant "be
sincere" to your own emotions which he muffles and fears. If I say
I hate that fellow (a friend of his) he bores me with his discreet
and nice words, he says I am displiant, that I should be nice to
everyone, which I don't understand because if you are nice and sweet
to all, you don't seem to me to discriminate and everyone is dumped
in the same category. I am for positive likes and negative dislikes,
I don't see how else you can live by the heart and the flesh otherwise. Here one must not show one's emotions or else people give
you a puzzled glance. Thus when I went to hear the Budapest
Quartet, a boy sitting by was annoyed because I kept keeping time
and moving my arms and head to the time of "Death and the
Maiden." Well, it is that savage, tropical light which seems here a
little too glaring. I keep remembering your image of reality scratch-
ing at my window on a cold day. She seems to say "let me in, boy."
But here people, I am afraid, live by another reality.

Did you read about the Western college, Wilmington, where
students and professors are working together on a dormitory for
nothing. A worthy cause! And the prof. of lit. said to the *Times*
reporter: Here between a "pass me another brick" and "give me a
hand with this wall" we discuss Hamlet and 19th century literary
trends. Pure and exhalting Ohio, n'est pas?[2]

Mother sold my two cows and sent me $200 last week. With the

2. The *New York Times* ran stories about the Quaker school, Wilmington College of Wilmington, Ohio, on Sunday and Monday, 14 and 15 November. José quotes Professor George Bowman of the English department.

money I bought a few books and went to the concert and the Princeton-Harvard game. Here you have a perfect example of dear Emerson's law of compensation. By the way, *Linda* our great Dane was lost or stolen a few weeks ago and mother has been very sad about it and writes me she has had two dreams in which she sees *Linda* locked up in the patio of Señora Consuelo, a lady she dislikes because she poisoned a cat of one of our neighbors and who, when mother's prize cock (a Plymouth Rock), named *Orlando,* named after my brother because he liked hens very much and was always running after our neighbor's, ran into her courtyard, she had the nerve to twist his neck and cook it up, sending mother the plumes and little legs (it was placed in our front door) as a warning. Well, mother has the obsession that the frightful woman has stolen *Linda* and locked her up as a revenge because Linda barks at night and keeps her awake. She doesn't dare go into Consuelo's yard to investigate the truthfulness of her 2 dreams but wants me to come home for Xmas to see to the matter. So the bitch's disappearance has become a major event in the family. Mother even threatens to go to the Police and denounce Consuelo. I had to write her a letter and told her to keep still until I arrive since it is not the first time she has been in Courts over her animals' welfare. Sometimes I wish she would sell all her beasts, for they give me considerable concern.

All this may seem to you very silly. But when these domestic quarrels and threats flow in from Habana, I forget Emerson, Garcilaso[3] and Eliot and get into a fit of despair.

I hope you are enjoying the blue skies and no clouds of smoke and cinder stifle your poetic existence in good old industrial Hartford. Here we have no shadows of any sort, everything is bathed in radiant, pure, aseptic light.

Yours,
José

3. Garcilaso de la Vega (1503–36), a lyric poet of the Spanish Golden Age.

[Princeton, New Jersey]
Nov. 18, 1948
Visperas de Dartmouth

My dear friend:

Your message of condolence[1] came and I was very amused at the thought, so I sent it to mother. I am sure she'll get a big kick out of it. She's very busy now; it seems some relative arrived two weeks ago from Vigo, and settled down in our small country house (where the menagerie is located). Mother, kind soul!, gave them the house and moved back to town. She says that these Spanish relatives landed with about five bottles of Málaga wine under their arms, *turrones* (candy from Gijón), and fifteen *chorrizos* (a sort of Spanish hot-dog, but bigger, heavier, and more *vital* looking). You make *ollas* and *pucheros* with these wonderful *chorrizos*—you add *berzas* (something like spinach sans the glamour of Popeye the sailor), *frijoles blancos,* chicken, ham (again the more realistic Spanish variety) and other ingredients. These *ollas* are called *potages* (French *potages?*) and it seems that the Spaniards to make the French term more peninsular or Imperial, if you please, make it an augmentative word and say *potajada,* which seems (the word I mean) to exude already the perfume and vitality of its many inherent virtues. It is like calling someone *bárbaro* (barbarian): in Spain a great compliment (or *piropo*). So to a great bullfighter one will yell "Bárbaro." I heard many times a Spanish poet refer to Cervantes as "ese bárbaro" (that barbarian). So if you call me *bárbaro,* I shall be pleased and never forget your enthusiasm and appreciation of my good virtues (Latin sense).

Well, the Spanish relatives have settled down with the Málaga wine, *chorrizos,* cheeses, etc., and are having a banquet, to which mother went, immediately invited, and had a hell of a time—eating, of course. For she is a great lover of food; she's rather heavy (I know) like Spanish ladies but with more of that pale, Mademoiselle Rubinstein soft looks. Rather more vital or musical and spiritual.

Saint Theresa, the great Spanish mystic, used to say *"Dios anda*

---

1. Stevens had sent a folded piece of paper simulating a commercial sympathy card, which carried a cartoon of Pluto and the words "Linda Requiescat! More later." (See photograph on page 104.)

entre mis pucheros" = "God is fooling around (or is) in my soup bowls."

This Spanish ability to unite the most sublime with the most lowly thoughts is something quite fascinating and of course mother is of the race.

2 hrs. later

It rains now. I am quite alone. I have been reading *The Courtier* of Castiglione, a delicious book which made me a little nostalgic for that court full of Italian ladies and gentlemen, for the Bembos, Gonzagos, Médicis, and Borjas. What an epoch! And then I look out of the window. It rains, still in stillness. And all about me, silence, sad grey silence. I don't wish another life, a romantic escapade into the Past; but it's just that the Castiglione made me a little homesick for some good substantial dialogue. And letters, scribbling away, one every once, now and then, are a poor antidote. Remember when you wrote of the "pressure" one must maintain to save the "noble" side of life against the furies of the other world? Or something like it![2] Well, in that tension one wastes away so many precious things, and misses so many precious meetings, encounters on the yard which never flower into a warm, sympathetic relation. God! Everyone is in such a hurry, here and there, back and forth, and where does it end, all? These things, and these half-awakened ephebes, who fly from their dreams to a lesson in history or geology and then back to their dreams and never feel or miss the fine sensations.

But enough!

I hope your letters won't be long in coming. Your thoughts have a fine nest here in 2 Dickinson. I pick them up, examine them carefully and usually they keep the little blood and spirit flowing. Without them, I feel a bit destitute and like giving up the whole farce. But that's not quite the whole picture, mind you! At times, I feel

2. "There is no element more conspicuously absent from contemporary poetry than nobility. . . . The mind has added nothing to human nature. It is a violence from within that protects us from a violence without. It is the imagination pressing back against the pressure of reality." "The Noble Rider and the Sound of Words," *NA*, 35–36.

very happy and know a warm handshake and affectionate pat on the shoulder and then moving away (for so we must) I pick up my courage and begin anew.

Your mandarin,
Joseito

[Hartford, Connecticut]
December 1, 1948

Dear José:

I am behind with letters, principally because I have had a lot of other things to do; and when I am busy a set of values engages me which is not the same set which engages me on holidays and bonfire nights. This sort of thing resembles the difference that exists between the state of mind of the writer and the state of mind of the reader. The two things do not co-exist. One writes for a week or two. Then one reads for a month or two. When I have been busy in the office, suddenly I feel that, important as all that is, I am after all losing time and then I read, and again, suddenly, I feel that reading is not enough and that it is time I collected myself and did a poem or two. Thus, the need for variety of experience asserts itself and the pressure of obscure cravings makes itself felt even here in Hartford, which is presumably an insensitive mass of insensitive people not to be thought of with Princeton (have you considered how pleasant it would be for you to know Frank Jewett Mather, Jr.)[1] or Havana where poets are like vines that bring color to the structure of the place out of the soil of Cuba or that country menage over which the Señora Consuelo presides with her malevolent shadow and influence. Even as she plots the purloining of Linda and meditates the suffocation of roosters she is confronted by the sounds and shouts of people from Vigo whom she is afraid even to abduct and imprison in her cellar, say, because there are so many of them and they are too jolly and too full of Malaga wine and cheese and, I hope, sausages.

Annyhoo,[2] I am not much worried right now by the fact that I

1. Frank Jewett Mather, Jr., was professor emeritus of art at Princeton.
2. This word was inadvertently corrected to "Anyhow" in *L,* 624.

know almost nothing of the thoughts of the early Christian fathers and expositors of Alexandria and so on. Last week I read a note on Valery in the October number of *French Studies*,[3] a periodical published by Blackwell in Oxford which I think you ought to look up because it makes Valery's skeleton ring, and yet as I read it I kept saying Who cares? Who the heck cares? One of the great spectacles in the world today is the flood of books coming from nothing and going back to nothing. This is due in part to the subjection of literature to money, in part to the existence of a lettered class to which literature is a form of self-indulgence. The savage assailant of life who uses literature as a weapon just does not exist, any more than the savage lover of life exists. Literature nowadays is largely about nothing by nobodies. Is it not so? What kind of book would that dazzling human animal Consuelo sit down to read after she had finished washing the blood off her hands and had hidden once more her machete in the piano? Will you write it for her? Sartre or Camus would if they had the time.

These stimulating suggestions are most inappropriate to the month of Christmas. Perhaps they are part of the revulsion I feel after looking through the book catalogues that have been coming in. Here one is in a fury to understand and to participate and one realizes that if there is anything to understand and if there is anything in which to participate one will pretty nearly have to make it oneself. Thus José stands up in his room at 2 Dickinson (as the clock strikes midnight and as Eliot and Blackmur step into their nightshirts and kneel down to say their prayers) and he creates by mere will a total wakefulness, brilliant in appearance, multi-colored, of which he is the dominant master and which he fills with words of understanding. Well, if he doesn't do it at 2 Dickinson, he may do it somewhere else. Bárbaro! Here the word shows its excellence. I suppose one never really writes about life when it is someone else's life, in the feeble laborious reportage of the student and artist. One writes about it when it is one's own life provided one is a good barbarian, a true Cuban, or a true Pennsylvanian Dutchman, in the linguistics of that soul which propriety, like another Consuelo, has converted into nothingness.

3. Henry Johnston, "A Note on Valéry," *French Studies* 2, no. 4 (October 1948): 333–40.

For the present there is little chance of seeing you in New York. My wife and I are going down this coming Friday but I already have several engagements and I shall have to spend a fair part of the time with her, with an occasional half hour out in a barber shop with hot towels on my imagination trying to forget it all. However, one does get home alive from such trips and out of all the forms one takes at such times one's self finally comes back and sits down and reads the *New Yorker* and says Hello yourself.

Be a good child as the scene becomes ice-bound. Let me have a few zips from your plume de Dimanche now and then.

Sincerely yours,
Wallace Stevens

[Princeton, New Jersey]
[3 December 1948]

My dear Voyant:

As Times flies the crow, I come to admire and fear you more and more. Your description of poor José in 2 Dickinson at twelve keeping vigil in wakefulness, waiting, oh, for the visitation of the spirits, will they come?, is so sadly true. How can you see into my mind and its workings from afar? Do I reveal so much in so little? Reading your letter I came to dwell on Thoreau, such a great poet, and his magnificent insight into natural objects. How can he describe accurately a minnow and turn it into a jewel of poetic beauty, gems almost Parnassian. What great men you had in those days! And I think how America has degenerated into a mess of Sun-Kiss oranges, A&P markets, Atomic professors who like Schubert's quartets for recreation after inventions, and Chinese-looking, elongated, white-skinned undergraduated gentlemen who assist at Liberal meetings and feel a nostalgia for the fast-running, hard-hitting quarter-backs! Oh, America betrayed by the Whitman and the Samuel Mayer (a Princeton prophet). How her savagery has been domesticated; that you miss and I don't understand at all. But you're a poet and I am just a candle burning at both ends and leaving only a few spots upon the carpets. I am sorry I won't see you sooner. I am going to Habana on the 18th. What would you like from the land of Consuelo and of so many consuelos to my tired, scholarly

[Princeton, New Jersey]

brain? What spoils can I deliver at your pine covered doorstep?

At present, I am watching with great concern the ripeness pro-
gressive with eyes voracious of a persimmon for I have never tasted
a Diospyros and would like to get my teeth into such a difficult
object. I went to a market with a friend, Schultz, who reads the
Spanish classics with ardour, so few like him here, and saw it, there
it stood in the splendour of its strange shape orange waiting for me
to discover it. So I took it home and here it rest on my study table
and I wonder if it (the persimmon) will fulfill my expectations,
it is "sweet and palatable when fully ripe." Like life. I hope after
a long vigil in which we insist in our anxiety of epiphanies. So I sit
and wait.

Eliot has left. I never saw him. He wrote but never beckoned me
to enter the forbidden den. I think it is to be blamed on a remark
I made at a cocktail party, I was drunk, about his perverse academic
attitude toward life. He would visit his old Prep School but was not
prepared to see anything or anyone that might disturb his Olympic
serenity. Because I suspect that the man is really a devil; he is possessed and has been kneeling in his night-shirt ever since he felt the
sting of the dart, in the hope of the thief who would come and rob
him of all his secret trade tricks. Like all great men he must shorten,
and oh how carefully, the leash lest his demon barks back at the
master. He has gone to Sweden where he will see beautiful blonde
figures skating upon ice and a benign, shrivelled old hand will
regally hand him a fat check and give him a little pat on the
shoulder.[1] How the vulgarization of literature reaches even the
damned poets! Imagine Rimbaud or Loutreamont Nobelized out of
existence! But such is modern life. Maybe the only escape is to
return to the mad, Bohemian days where poets dressed like dandies
and threw stones at the crystal mansions of the fat bourgeoise.
Burgueses y mas burgueses!

I met John Berryman, a mad chap, why? Well, I heard him
recite Pound with a fervour and I was moved. I admire him then.
I don't like his poetry, but I think he reads Pound (recites Pound)

1. Compare José's vision of Eliot accepting the Nobel Prize with Eliot's
own: Asked to crown the Swedish snow queen at the winter festival, Eliot
told Robert Giroux that he had hoped this might be combined with the
Nobel ceremony, so that he could wear ice skates with his tails. Unpublished letter paraphrased by Ackroyd, *T. S. Eliot,* 289–90, 360 n. 56.

like he deserves with a sort of fanatical entonation. Who is Frank Mather? Does it mathers that I should know him?

Mother writes that she is fattening the pig (we eat pig sans the apple not Turkeys at home) and she is happy yes because soon we shall be looking for Linda. The bibijaguas (big ants that eat everything in sight when they are really hungry which is a very logical procedure I think) have eaten up her best roses. She wants me to do something about them too. She has a theory that they leave their underground home every seven years; a theory she probably got from her Bible-reading years. Anyways, the bibijaguas are there waiting for me. When I enter the garden I am sure they will all turn their little shiny black heads around and murmur to each other, "He must be the one she has talked so much about. It's time we get back home". And everything will be alright.

I wish you would send me the article on Valery. I cannot find it here. Princeton's library is very poor. Mostly scientific, political, and economic nonsense.

Pierre Emmanuel, the French Catholic poet, gave a talk all about anguish, suffering, the Cruxificion and Ressurection(?), and I was much amused to see the expressions on the men of letters' snouts as they heard him undress his soul and told what made his poetry tick. It was like seeing one of those wonderful Parisian performers in those circuses you see in the dirty smelly suburbs of the English capital or a seal making a dive and coming out of the water applauding with her two pretty rear hands, a herring in her mouth! I enjoyed it. Although I understand the Americans' distaste.[2] Rousseau was born in France, I remembered.

It is three o'clock. I must say good-night. I hope you will zip your plume soon.

The persimmon still looks promising,
José

2. The difficulty of finding Valéry at Princeton may have reminded José here of the lecture by Pierre Emmanuel, for the French poet probably mentioned Valéry in the performance that so offended; Emmanuel's own poetry had been profoundly influenced by Valéry's La Jeune Parque. The two books of poems Emmanuel wrote while working with the French Resistance were intended, according to the poet, to express intense suffering and raise pain to an absolute. Emmanuel maintained a prophetic tone, mingling erotic and Catholic imagery. At the time of the lecture he was working for the North American service of the French radio.

[Hartford, Connecticut]
December 14, 1948

Dear José:

There isn't a thing in Cuba that I want. But perhaps I ought not to let you go without wishing you a Merry Christmas and expressing the hope that you will enjoy the Linda Brand of frankfurters, which are, I understand, something new in the Havana market, with a comparatively limited supply. Also, I want to suggest that if you return by way of New York you visit the gallery of Pierre Matisse and see the pictures by Jean Dubuffet.[1] These are the most potent things I have seen for a long time: horrible but at the same time potent with the effort of an extraordinarily intelligent man to arrive at the source of art in the mind. Jean Dubuffet goes to Africa in the winter and there he and his wife and his children, or at least one child, live on the desert, in a tent, with the Arabs. A friend of his told me this. And there in the desert he struggles against everything that he has picked up at home in an effort to arrive at what he himself is and what he himself sees, feels and thinks. You can tell Mari[an]o about these pictures when you see him at home.

I suppose you will be back after the holidays and will make a little report.

Sincerely yours,
Wallace Stevens

[Princeton, New Jersey]
Dec. 15 [1948]

My dear friend:

I am about to take the jump; mother will be waiting at the other air-end with the whole menangerie. Since the snow has ruined the Princeton landscape, the escape comes very timely, indeed.

I am still with a hang-over from the big party I went to, yesterday, to celebrate my birth-day, the purple 28th. I was born, I could point out now, on Dec. 14; same day when San Juan de La Cruz died in Ubeda (1591). Amen.

1. Jean Dubuffet, painter and sculptor, born in 1901. His mixed media sculptures, including "Cow with the Subtile Nose" and "Beard of Uncertain Return," were on exhibit at the Museum of Modern Art.

I shall look into the gallery Matisse; never heard you so exultant about a painter hereto; must look them up!

I don't know if I wrote you of my plans to study at the Univ. of Madrid next Fall. I'll try very hard to convince my family that it is a thing worthwhile; I want very much to go abroad before the atoms break loose again and nothing is left but the Caves of Almeria, with their prints of primitive men in their rocks, to reveal again the vanity of men and things.

Yours in the Epiphany,
José

[Hartford, Connecticut]
January 27, 1949

Dear José:

Since I was in New York last Saturday (January 22) I could not very well come down on the 5th. A later occasion will have to do. I found it very worth while, *alone,* last week. There is an exhibition of things by Piranesi at the Morgan Library which you ought to see. Besides, you ought to see Morgan Library. Be sure to go through the corridor which runs off from the place of the exhibition into the sanctuaries beyond. The main stack contains endless incunabula and since you may come to spend your life with such things you had better take a look at this particular collection, even though you can only read the titles through the grilles. Your secret self will be enriched. Also in that main room there is a case containing an exhibition of memorabilia related to Charles I of England, including one piece that exhibits his attitude toward the people on the edge of the scaffold. I was shocked to find that it was also your attitude and mine. I was particularly shocked to find that it was mine. I side irresistably with the aristocracy of the good and the wise and I am quite sure that I, too, ought to be beheaded. I don't know that Charles I limited his sense of the divine right of kings to himself, but there are certain definite kings for whose divine right I am prepared to see at least your head, if not my own, roll at the feet of the populace. But who is good and who is wise . . . . . ? At the Buchholz Gallery there is a collection of sculptures by Jean Arp.[1]

1. Jean (or Hans) Arp (1887–1966), French painter and sculptor.

Arp exists in the atmosphere of modern art if not exactly on its plane. He is too much a man of taste to be a leader, like Picasso. Yet he is exquisite and you should see his work.

I thought the last number of *Orígenes* an exceptional one.[2] Of course I can only drift through it in my ignorance of the lingo. But what an idea: that one about the psychology of the horse. The truth is that I have an overwhelming number of new things to read and am beginning to feel like throwing a dust cover over the whole lot. I am not willing to spend so much time reading when there is so much thinking and writing and running about New York to do!

Stay put and I shall let you know sometime when I am coming down. After all, Princeton is only a fraction of the distance from New York that Hartford is.[3]

Sincerely yours,
Wallace Stevens

[Princeton, New Jersey]
[January 1949]

Mi dear Don Walacio:

I am certain some wizard or mage took my letter to your castle and flew back, presto!, thru the clouds. And since I am reading Don Quijote, passionately, I have a tendency to see in events and appearances the working of some "encantador." You must remember that every time the Don was defeated, like when he attacked the sheeps, and Sancho reasons that they were only sheeps and not an army of caballeros, he says: Some wizard has turned them to sheeps to rob me of the glory due to such a valiant knight as I. Well, it is all marvelously true. And you only have to *believe* like Don Quijote and it will be true! It is strange indeed how upon reading the book again I come to *live* it; something quite impossible to do if you read it when you are young and have not suffered the trial of fire and water. Sometimes, I am so moved that I feel like crying. Which might seem silly to you. But I am still a sentimental creature and

2. The issue contained articles by Lezama Lima, García Vega, and Cintio Vitier, among others.
3. The fraction is not as small as Stevens suggests; Hartford is only forty-five miles further from New York.

hope to God shall never my veins and arteries turn to stone and certain sights won't anymore bring a sigh.

In N.Y. I saw Talullah;[1] "Summer and Smoke"; next Saturday will see "A Streetcar Named Desire." I like Tennessee Williams' plays, since I find in his works certain fire and poetry which no other American playwright concerns himself with. Went to Rosenberg and saw some beautiful still-lifes: a lovely delicate Picasso and a really wonderful Bracque. Try to see them. I shall go and look at the sights you recommend.

Suzanne Langer spoke here on Symbols and more symbols. She had a pretty definition of Art Expression. After the lecture I went to the forum and asked her a few questions about poetry and especially St. John of the Cross. She was very crossed with me and told me she didn't understand what I was trying to say to her. I felt humiliated and left her with [a] mouth full of symbols. I do believe she is very intelligent, but sort of frustrated and too smart for her feminine desires. Like a Spaniard, I reasoned she would be more useful in the kitchen making pies or trying her hand at a fricase de guineas.

I read today of the death of Theodore Spencer;[2] at the same time I saw a little verse of his, postumo, in the *New Yorker* (I think). I was quite amazed: he died of a heart attack in a cab: a very sordid death for a man who dwelled among the Greeks, liked beautiful women and a dozen Martinis on the weekend. I liked him very much when I was at Cambridge: seeing in him the perfect blend of the gentleman and the scholar.

I hope you let me know ahead of time next time you plan to go into N.Y. It is very strange but Saturday the 22 I went to the bar of the Sherry-Netherland because I remembered you had made an appointment for us to meet there and since then I always look with approval and enjoy drinking there.

> Yours with magic,
> Don José

1. José may have seen Tallulah Bankhead or a "Tallulah" type in the audience for *Summer and Smoke*. Coincidentally, she was in a revival of *A Streetcar Named Desire* two years later.

2. The critic and poet died on 18 January 1949. He had attained the rank of associate professor of English at Harvard during the years José was a student there.

Jan 26 [1949]

My dear Mr. Stevens:

I'm back—and alive! I have a few days off. Could I see you in N.Y. sometime before Feb. 7. Then classes begin again. That's if you happen to be going there in that interval.

I wish I could write you of my "aventuras" home. Mother however is rather nervous & I have been worrying & wondering if she will really be sick or not. So I let that pass for the time being.

Do answer.

Yours affectionately,
José

[Princeton, New Jersey]
Feb. 3, 1949

My dear Arp-Deceiver:

I went to N.Y. just as I said and took a good look at Arpie; but I came back very disappointed. I guess that sort of Latin's delicacy is too much for us South of the Border. I found M. Arp geometrical a las Descartes, but who cares for French precision, classicism, razon. I took off to a little bar on second Avenue and got drunk.

Tomorrow I am "journeying" to Baltimore to see a friend and expect, if Time permits, to look at a wonderfully oldish and illuminating exhibition of rare books. I expect you know all about them, by now. Speaking of jewels, I saw you endorsing a book on a similar subject by a Mr. Downing[1] of Partisan. Is it worthwhile? I am very depressed: I finished Don Quijote. No more adventures, no more wizards, no more life. I am now settling down to write a little essay: Upon reading the Quijote for the "first" time. Maybe I can translate it into English and send it to you. Eh?

I have been reading a little of Thurber; I find him very funny, strangely as it may seem, a la Cervantes. I don't (so peculiarly American) suppose he is rated very high by the "critics" but it seems to me he has it over many serious boys who are struggling

1. José means Allan Dowling, who was raising money for the *Partisan Review* and had solicited Stevens' help in October 1948. Stevens told Barbara Church that while he disagreed with its politics, he thought the group "well worth helping"; see *L*, 620. See also letter of 15 December 1947, n. 1.

very hard with Lady Literature. SUR in its issue dedicated to American lit. had a story of Mr. Thurber, but that may be another instance of Senora Ocampo's snobbism.[2] Did you see Delmore's piece on Eliot in the last Partisan?[3] The title is very typical of his subtle kind of humour. I met a Jew in N.Y. who spoke of Matisse and Picasso in terms analogous and I never have been so amused and impressed by anyone else who has looked and felt entitled to say profound niceties of these two great painters.

I am hoping to go West next Spring. I have just received a long letter from a friend I thought dead; he wants me to visit him in San Diego. So I may journey there and take in the California landscape.

I hope to write you soon and tell you about Catholic Baltimorians. Until then I remain yours sans Arp,

José

[Hartford, Connecticut]
March 9, 1949

Dear José:

I have not forgotten you but it has just not been possible for me to write letters recently. I like to write letters in spare moments at the office. There have been no spare moments.

My next trip to New York will be next Thursday, March 17th, but I shall be busy downtown until early afternoon and shall then have many personal odds and ends to take care of before running to the train. After that I do not expect to be in New York until April 18th, when I shall stay overnight. However, April 18th falls on Monday. I should like very much to see you again, particularly so if you are still thinking of going to Madrid in the autumn. I shall be immensely interested in arranging for a series of postcards, etc. from Madrid. Seriously, I cannot imagine anything more interesting than to know someone there and through that person to acquire some sense of the place. If we have not seen one another by about a month before you start south, let me know and I shall come down

2. "Fabulas Para Nuestro Tiempo" (Stories for Our Time), 14 (March–April 1944): 261–64.
3. "The Literary Dictatorship of T. S. Eliot," *Partisan Review* 16, no. 2 (February 1949): 119–37.

specially some Saturday and we can have lunch and perhaps a little talk. I might be able to tempt Delmore Schwartz and perhaps one or two others to join us. I have not seen Delmore Schwartz for more than a year; in fact, I have seen no-one in New York.

This spring I have had quite a number of invitations to talk here and there but I don't see the connection between writing poetry and delivering lectures. I am not a lecturer and I have no intention of doing that sort of thing except in cases in which I very much want to. It would be interesting to meet people in colleges, but then one never meets them at a lecture. If, for example, General Eisenhower should ask me to come down to Columbia and have a few highballs with him, that would be worth while. Yet it may be that, even if he did, when I got down there he would want to show me moving pictures of Hitler's funeral or something.

Good luck my tropical amigo. I mean well but a widower with six children or a cat with twelve kittens has nothing on me.

Sincerely yours,
Wallace Stevens

The Nassau Club
Princeton, N.J.
March 11, [19]49

Albricias Don Gualacio!

I was happy to hear from you again; I hope we shall see each other in April. I could come on the 18th of April (Monday) as I don't have classes until Tuesday at 2:20 P.M. If you could tell me ahead of time where you are staying the evening of the 18th, I might get reservations there myself. That's if you are not going to be so busy on the 18th that we couldn't sit down for a talk or go for a walk together. If you prefer to go into N.Y. some Saturday in May, it's fine but as I say I shall be free to join you in April.

At present, I am relaxing after passing my Oral Exams in Spanish literature. Reading E. R. Curtius' *Essai sur la France,*[1] Husserl and Spanish poetry.

1. Possible titles: *The Civilization of France,* Introduction by Ernst R. Curtius, translated by Olive Wyon (London: G. Allen and Unwin, 1932), or *L'Idée de civilisation dans la conscience française,* translated from the

Mother writes that Violeta, her black and white cow, gave birth to a fine, all black *ternero* (young bull). She is painting the country house and incubating many new chicks. All goes well there. My brother's wife is coming north to have her third baby. Mother calls her *gata* (female cat) because like the cats she has an offspring every spring season.

Cuba is ready to break off with Russia because some Cuban *gracioso* had the funny idea of making and wearing a mask of Stalin during the carnivals to scare girls off. They could not discover who was behind the big mustache, but everyone had lots of fun with the mask and the Russian delegation protested violently. Cuba's sense of humor was too much for them, and there we are. All sounds like opera buffa which Cubans are too apt to turn life into quite frequently. I am sorry however because when I went to the Russian parties I had a wonderful time, eating caviar, drinking champagne and discussing Cuba's latest painter or poet and hearing the Russians' viewpoint on the matter. Cuban intellectuals will miss the Russian parties. I couldn't say the same for the American embassy's parties where everyone drinks whiskey and talks business or politics.

Do write soon and let me know where you are staying on the 18th and if my coming up will fit in with your schedule. Otherwise, I hope we can arrange something in May. I go back to paradise around June the 3rd.

Yours sincerely,
José

P.S. Has the poem, "The Novel," appeared yet? Have you seen Mr. Eliot's pretentious little essay on Kultur?[2] There is a very amusing article in this week's *New Yorker* on Sidney Frankly,[3] the American toreador. Don't miss it!

German by Henri Jourdan (Paris: Association for International Conciliation, 1939).

2. T. S. Eliot's "Notes toward the Definition of Culture" appeared in *Partisan Review* 11, no. 2 (Spring 1944): 145–57. In addition, Eliot's essay "What Is a Classic" appeared in a Spanish translation in *Sur* 153, no. 16 (July 1947): 18–44.

3. Sidney Franklin is the subject of the first of a three-part essay in the *New Yorker* by Lillian Ross, "El Unico Matador," 12 through 26 March 1949.

[Hartford, Connecticut]
March 14, 1949

Dear José:

The date in April, Easter Monday, is the date of what is called
the Paas Festival of the St. Nicholas Society of which I am a pious
member.[1] I am coming down in order to go to that dinner. Now,
if you would like to go along, I should be glad to arrange it. You
have to dress for it and I have no idea whether you have dinner
clothes with you or not. It isn't very funny but it is rather nice.
Everyone there is supposed to be descended from 17th or 18th
Century residents of New York City. I shall be very glad to have
you as my guest if you want to go. I should have to let you know
later about where I am going to stay because I don't know myself
right now and we could then arrange a meeting.

On the other hand, on some other occasion I might be able to
get a few friends together. In any case, even if I did not succeed, we
could do as we pleased: have a pleasant dinner somewhere.

In the same mail with your letter I received a letter from a man
in Ceylon with whom I have been carrying on correspondence for
some years. Note the date of his letter. It used to take about six
weeks in each direction for an exchange of letters. As the date of
his letter shows, it takes just about a week nowadays. This man is
an Oxford man who has lived in Ceylon all his life. He is the
descendant of one of the early Dutch settlers out there. Please
return this letter. I thought you might be interested in seeing it.[2]

Sincerely yours,
Wallace Stevens

1. See letter of 8 January 1948, n. 5.
2. Leonard C. Van Geyzel dated his letter to Stevens 5 March. Van
Geyzel thanked Stevens for having sent the posthumous *Collected Essays*
of John Peale Bishop (1948) as a Christmas gift, yet indicated several
flaws, one being Bishop's "uncritical" essay on *Gone with the Wind,* which
seemed to Van Geyzel an "alarming instance of Southern myopia." Stevens
knew José would also appreciate Van Geyzel's explanation of the difficulty
of translating and then broadcasting Eliot's Sweeney in Sinhalese, a project
for which Eliot had given Van Geyzel permission. "Sweeney for instance
will have to be read," Van Geyzel explained, "while Sinhalese verse is
always sung." Huntington Library manuscript.

[José and Stevens met in New York, as scheduled, on Monday, 18 April.]

[Hartford, Connecticut]
April 22, 1949

Dear José:

I enclose a letter to Mr. Knopf. You can send this to him and ask for an appointment. My own guess would be that the right approach would be through Herbert Weinstock. Of course Mr. Knopf is the works but whether you could interest him offhand in a translation of 17th Century Spanish comedy, even if it was as funny as Mrs. Astor's goat, remains to be seen. After all, if you are seriously trying to place a book you have to think about how to go about it. If you try to tell these people about Roja, they are going to say that the man has been dead for 200 or 300 years. You will have to think it out from that point on for yourself.

Do you know anything about Dudley Fitts? He is a teacher. Just where he teaches at the moment I don't know. He is about as keen as they come concerning words and ideas. My own belief about Fitts is that if he could get hold of the right material and let himself go completely, it would be the making of him. If you are going to associate anyone with you in the translation of "La Celestina," think twice about associating a professor. It would be a thousand times better for you to associate someone like Fitts who would frolic all over the place and enrich the text with all kinds of enjoyments of his own with your help.[1]

Moreover, what would Knopf or Weinstock say if you tried to interest either of them in a translation that has not yet actually been made. Publishing a book is a piece of business. If you could go to Knopf and lay the translation on his desk and associate a good man

1. That José knew and corresponded with Dudley Fitts is confirmed in a letter José wrote to Allen Tate (15 February [1949], Tate Papers, Princeton University Library). For many years Fitts was master in English at the Choate School in Wallingford, Connecticut, which José attended. Undoubtedly he was familiar with Fitts' *Anthology of Contemporary Latin-American Poetry* (Norfolk, Conn.: New Directions, 1947). By 1949 Fitts was teaching at Phillips Academy in Andover, Massachusetts.

with you, someone really capable of dazzling him, and Fitts is just
that, and if at the same time you could say that if Knopf published
the book the theatre at Princeton would produce the play, you
would have something to sell.

I am returning Santayana's letter. Your devotion to this superb
figure delights me. How strong his handwriting is and how the
whole letter convinces one that there is nothing mixes with long
life like a strong mind. I love his remark: "I have always, somewhat
sadly, bowed to expediency or fate."

Sincerely yours,
Wallace Stevens

[Hartford, Connecticut]
April 22, 1949

Dear Mr. Knopf:

I am writing to introduce José Rodríguez-Feo, a young man from
Havana, who wants to try to interest you in something that I know
nothing about. But I do know him personally and, regardless of
anything else, I think that you would enjoy meeting him and that
it might turn out to be of value. He has asked me to introduce him
to you, which I am sincerely glad to do.

Sincerely yours,
Wallace Stevens

[Princeton, New Jersey]
[April or May, 1949]

My dear Poeta:

I hope you have not frozen up there! I have just passed my Oral
Exams. They gave me to choose ten themes; I could pick one—
I did [Antonio] Machado, a modern Spanish poet—and they asked
me to discuss a second theme which I was not to know. For the 2nd
they asked me to discuss [Pedro] Calderón's *Life is a Dream.* Well,
that's over!

Yesterday, Princeton celebrated its Junior Prom, quite a feast.
Drunk young men all over the prematurely verdant campus, jig-
gling Vassar gals, etc. All very gay and collegiate!

I am still looking forward to seeing you in NYC some day before I go home in June.

> Yours ever,
> José

[Hartford, Connecticut]
May 11, 1949

Dear José:

Can you have lunch with me in New York on Thursday, May 19th? If this is convenient, I shall look for you in the lobby at the Passy on East 63rd Street between Park and Madison at 12:45.

> Sincerely yours,
> Wallace Stevens

[Undoubtedly José wrote or phoned to apologize for missing their appointment on the nineteenth.]

[Hartford, Connecticut]
June 1, 1949

Dear José:

Instead of being annoyed, the truth is that I had intended to take you to a party where there were quite a lot of people that you would have enjoyed meeting. I was too busy thinking about the party both before it occurred and afterward to think about being annoyed. I have not written to you because I thought that it might really be necessary to forego seeing you and I thought of leaving it to chance. I never know when I am going to New York and at the moment have no present plans for going at all. Nothing would please me more than to see you here. There is an excellent train from New York at 9:10 which arrives in Hartford at 11:39, both d.s.t. This would be just right for lunch. We could go over to the Canoe Club, with which you are familiar,[1] and then no doubt you could pick up

---

1. José's familiarity with the Canoe Club provides the only confirmation in the letters of his visit to see Stevens in Hartford. Their luncheon "on the *orilla* of the river that runs through that city" had probably taken place in 1948. José Rodríguez Feo to Alan Filreis, 29 May 1984.

some train for Boston although you had better look that up. The trains from Hartford to Boston pass through Wellesley although they don't all stop there, especially after the girls have left when there is practically no reason at all for stopping.

I shall be delighted to see you here and to hear about your plans. You keep me young.

Sincerely yours,
Wallace Stevens

[Hartford, Connecticut]
June 9, 1949

Dear José:

I am sorry that I shall not be seeing you for the present. We have had a week of the most perfect Cuban weather here in Hartford. But I cannot say that one is free any longer to go on enjoying the weather in June. Politics is in everything. This morning I received a notice of a meeting of the Phi Beta Kappa. I enclose part of the notice saying who was to be orator and whose name is x'd out. So that the sextons of liberty at Washington horn in even on the meetings of Phi Beta Kappa. Judith Coplon and Alexander Palmer and Mr. Chambers and Mr. Hiss all give me a prolonged pain in the neck.[1] I wish I could forget all about them when I am taking my walk in the park in the mornings by sitting down and having a little talk with the ducks, but I am sure that the ducks are Russian spies. It would almost be a relief if someone blew hell out of everything. In an effort to prove that everything that has been wrong has been wrong, what really has been accomplished is the establishing of the fact that everything that is is nuts. The Canoe Club was built for just this purpose and I am going there for lunch today. Yet you can see how dreadfully wrong everything is from this: last night we had some strawberries after dinner. They were

1. Predating, and somewhat rivaling, the Hiss-Chambers espionage trials was the arrest and eventual conviction of Judith Coplon, daughter of a wealthy toy manufacturer and a graduate of Barnard College, on charges of passing FBI and Justice Department papers to a Russian engineer employed at the United Nations. Archibald (not Alexander) Palmer was her attorney.

the most perfect berries in the world but the only sugar available was brown *health* sugar. Oh my god! Misericorde and misericorde.

Be sure to send me a postcard or two from your turquoise hostel *la bas.*

Very sincerely yours,
Wallace Stevens

THE PLANET PANCREAS

1949–1951

In the summer of 1949 José suffered a
severe case of colitis and returned to Havana, where despite bad
health he was for the most part content to remain. The illness
caused him to miss out on a job offer at Princeton that fall, and
except for a few months' visit to the campus, José stayed in Cuba
to become "quite a businessman," as he overstates it to his Yankee
mentor.

Stevens reached seventy years old during this period and tried to
answer some of José's talk of physical and emotional isolation with
matter of factness—an account of a last visit he had with a dying
peer, personal thoughts on the death of Theodore Spencer. His late,
rich collection, *The Auroras of Autumn* (1950), which contained
"The Novel," was published in this period; he no doubt treasured
the idea of José reading the book at his family's sugar plantation
and then arranging an evening with his young friends in which José
offered them spontaneous translations of favorite poems.

In every letter now, José urged Stevens to come to Havana where
he would be warmly received by everyone from José's mother and
sister to the admiring Lezama Lima, whose prize-winning book of
poems, *La fijeza* (1949), some believe is full of Stevensean echoes.
Meanwhile, between bouts of "intestinal affliction" of one kind or
another and more difficulties with his mother's mental health, José
continued to work on his literary projects. The wide and fruitful
range of his interests continued to produce a lively correspondence.

Both men by now had come to admire each other's talent for a
certain "monotony of elegance" and to depend upon news of the
particular form it takes in their separate spheres.

[Hartford, Connecticut]
July 29, 1949

Dear José:

Your postcard from Varadero Beach is on my dresser at home,
where the surf of it rolls day and night making mild Cuban sounds.
I am not sure whether you are there or in Havana, so that I am
addressing this to Havana.

What has meant most to me recently has been the visit of Dr.
Schweitzer. The trouble with this figure is that one does not associate it with anything except an ant-proof organ on the equator and
a pair of mustaches like African ferns. And, while Schweitzer is
regarded as a philosopher, one does not really feel that he is a
thinker, though he may be. One associates him with his life, not
with his ideas. His life is only one of many. The awe-inspiring
powers to think, study logically, penetratingly (which is what you
experience after you have had a drink at the Club Kawama) until
one's head is like an object crawling with big Cuban lightning bugs
is not exactly common-place. Anyhow, even limited to his life,
without the rationalizing that lies back of it and even if, then, he is
no more magnificent than any missionary, religious, medical, political, or economic, he is still magnificent: an eminent figure of
non-self-seeking in a world in which self-seeking is as prevalent
as breathing.

Midsummer is a suffocating time and I long, not for Cuba, but
for a cottage, say, in Sweden on a lake surrounded by dark green
forests in which all the trees talk Swedish. The repetition of one's
experiences in a single spot year after year is deadly. But, then, so
too is a life without the need of a job and without the plans that
one is constantly making to amuse oneself. Even the scholar must
have a subject for his life and however suffocating this time of year
may be it has always been a time when I am happiest, as if the
world had become composed at last.

Today I had lunch at the Canoe Club, with three Martinis. Richard Eberhart of Cambridge was here a week or two ago and I took him there. From him I was able to find out something about the death of Theodore Spencer. It seems that Spencer had had a heart attack a year ago. Thus he must have known when the fatal attack came on how serious the situation was. When the taxi stopped in front of his house and the driver opened the door, Spencer's big foot fell out. While I never knew him well, I wish I had. We came from the same part of the world. We must have had much in common. And one is always desperately in need of the fellowship of one's own kind. I don't mean intellectual fellowship, but the fellowship of one's province: membership in a clique, the fellowship of the landsman and compatriot.

I am sending you a clipping from a feuilleton by [V. S.] Pritchett who has moved into the country in England.[1] I thought that the final touch about flies would interest you. If the influence of flies is as consequential as all that, then perhaps what is disturbing the world today is fleas. I don't mean the homely Russian fleas, but the gypsy fleas of Roumania and the barbaric buggers of Bulgaria. If Pritchett is right about the flies, isn't it possible that Communism is the result of fleas. Certainly that would explain its miraculous diffusion. Moreover, if there is anything to this theory, the democratic nations are in real danger since they have nothing with which to fight back except the Japanese beetle and the boll-weevil, unless you have something in Cuba, particularly in the beds of the country hotels, that would help. And I don't mean cockroaches.

Well, José, genial professor, spirit of learning, artist of Kawama, there you are. As you see, my interior world is in great disorder, wishing you the same; but in all this heat anything else would be an affectation. I continue to seek wisdom and understanding and

1. *"Why Do I Write?" An Exchange of Views between Elizabeth Bowen, Graham Greene, and V. S. Pritchett* (London: P. Marshall, 1948). In the first letter, to Elizabeth Bowen, Pritchett describes a visit to an agricultural fair in Lichfield; his animated comments on the barnyard sights and smells may have recalled to Stevens' mind José's description of the activity in his own barnyard. The letter is a short essay on the relation between the artist's imagination and the society in which he lives, focusing on three statues Pritchett encountered in Lichfield: George Fox, the Quaker apologist; Samuel Johnson, looking "puddingy, porridgy"; and a rakish Boswell, "a greater writer than either, vain as a dragon fly."

wish it were possible to do so in New York occasionally, but New York at the moment is hotter than Alexandria, and, as the Chinaman said of the United States, too full of foreigners. Here in Hartford we have the advantage of receiving postcards, and doing whatever there is to do in air-conditioned circumstances.

Greetings, best wishes and au revoir.

Sincerely yours,
Wallace Stevens

[Jose's reply, probably another postcard, has been lost.]

[Hartford, Connecticut]
October 28, 1949

Dear José:

I am glad to hear that you are only half dead. The truth is that I thought either that your mother was ill or that you were or that you had departed for Madrid. My guess is, however, that it is much nicer to plan to depart for Madrid than actually to do so.

I should not grieve too much about the loss of your job at Princeton. No doubt you will be able to get it back. Anyhow, providence may have invented colitis and such things for the purpose of preventing promising young Cubans, say, from becoming school teachers. I realize that a spirit like yours, panting for the company of the erudite and wise, finds an overwhelming attraction in merely being in such places as Princeton and Cambridge, etc., which are so lousy with the erudite and wise. Providence has, as I say, probably invented colitis so that you could sit on the front porch and respond to Cuba and make something of it, and help to invent or perfect the idea of Cuba in which everyone can have a being just as everyone has a special being in a great church—in the presence of any great object. Your job is to help to create the spirit of Cuba. Every one of your friends who writes a poem, whether or not it is about Cuba which nevertheless is a thing of the place, and every one of your friends who does a painting which in a perfectly natural way is a particular thing as a sapodilla is, or a good fat cigar or a glass of piña fria is, is doing just what you ought to be doing somehow or other.

This same subject has been in my mind in another form in the last few days. I have been reading a book of short stories by an Irishman.[1] The best one of the lot is about a romantic Irish liar in a barroom who tells someone else who enters the bar about his experiences as a lion tamer. Once every so often he says "At last, Ireland has produced a lion tamer." Why should Cuba produce a youth who teaches at Princeton? Why should it not produce someone who is her own son who not only looks it but is it, just the way Ireland ought to produce not lion tamers but sons who look it and are it? My stenographer tells me that I have these pronouns all balled up. Excuse handwriting.

Well, if you ever get out of that rocking chair and come to New York, let me know and I shall be glad to come down.

Apparently Allen Tate is teaching at Princeton this year, but he has written to say that he is in New York several days a week.

I am planning to have another book, the way a woman plans to have quadruplets.[2] I have the greatest ambitions for this next book, but at my age one's ambitions rarely realize themselves: quadruplets turn out to be triplets.

I don't know of any other news. We have not yet had a real frost here. It looked like it here this morning but it was largely due to the fact that the ground was damp. Some of our roses have gone limp. It has not been bitter enough yet to knock them out. If we should have a warm week or two, no one would know the difference. But we are not likely to have a warm week or two. The moon which moves around over Havana these nights like a waitress serving drinks moves around over Connecticut the same nights like someone poisoning her husband.

Sincerely yours,
Wallace Stevens

1. Bryan MacMahon, *The Lion Tamer and Other Stories* (New York: Dutton, 1949).

2. The manuscript of *The Auroras of Autumn* was ready in early January.

All Saints' Day

My dear Wallacho:

Your letter came in a most propitious moment: to the accords of Haydn and when I was savouring a lovely poem of Quevedo, "Al Ruiseñor." I am simply amazed at your long-distance intuitions. If I do go to Princeton it is to be surrounded by a cold wind, books, intellectual surprises. I realize there is little wisdom and much erudition. But then in Habana there is only a mask of wisdom and no erudition. There is however the possibility, oh so delicious, of finding friends with refined erudition, like you, that is men who have made of their knowledge something vital, almost poetic in their internal form. I see that here all people, myself after a while, invent diversions to "kill time," that is to kill themselves. And the anguish remains: the realization that after all one *cannot* live at the peak or "cumulus" of intensity. That life must be dull, monotonous, if then, later, we are to enjoy moments of excitement or discover a mysterious relation between the quotidian and the marvelous. But if you are not prepared, and I thought I was, to accept life as something shot with dull moments, and the notion, Christian?, that for a moment of joy there are ten of boredom, much more horrible than suffering, or perhaps the acutest form of personal suffering—then one is very unhappy. I have been always rather unhappy and alone. But who will give in? I thought I could. That is to say, accept daily existence as something casual, to dispense with as one does with the frijoles or the newspaper, as it comes. But I have become violently intolerant, not of people, but of moments that do not offer me what I desire. Not always sensual pleasure although everything for me revolves around a sensual instinct but a sort of pleasure *in* life and *with* life. What I can call an aesthetics of life. Everything seems to conspire, my colitis included, against such an aesthetics. If I have colitis, I cannot find pleasure in a cup of jerez or manzanilla; or I am told not to dance because I might get "excited" and that heat would disturb my sensitive colon. Etc. You see what I mean, I hope. Then a life of reclusion, absorbed in thoughts and meditations is fine but I want a change, once in a while. The trip to Spain, which you seem to deprecate, seems such a nice change! Another *paisaje,* another people to look at with curiosity and "enamoured eyes in an icy face". Something to ruminate on when I return to the tropics. I think I would really enjoy Spain because there I believe I would discover new ways of looking at things and persons. There are many ways of looking just as there are many ways of *not* looking. This look, or gazing at objects, is what Mr. Bewley[1] does not see in your poems, because his approach is not, as should be wherever you have a poem, an amorous one. There is no delectation in his look. That is why he entertains himself in resolving the logical processes of an idea or image in your poetry, in seeing who is Azcan or the meaning of the Capitan or the proliferation of the sombrero. Yet, the essay seems to me the most interesting thing that has been written about your poetry. But so much is left out. Perhaps, things cannot be described for to do so one would have to write another poem or re-create the thoughts and the feelings that permeate the act of composition. The more I read critiques of poetry, the more I come to understand the futility of such [a] task.

I am going to a jai alai game with a friend who does not like poetry so I shall continue tomorrow. Adios.

After the jai alai game I went down with the grippe toxic. It is the fashion here now. Everybody has the grippe. So I delayed the envoy of this correspondence. Lezama was very pleased with your message of congratulations on the coming out of his book, *La Fijeza*.[2] He was delighted you discovered affinities with your poetry in "Variations on a Tree".

The isle is really wonderful now. There is a constant cold wind stroking our palm trees; the skies cover themselves with lovely blue shades and the sunsets are something to look at. I don't understand why you don't take a trip down here one of these days. My trip to Spain has been postponed because there are several family businesses in the oven, and I want to be here to see how they are cooked. I am thinking of selling all our stocks in the sugar business. I am of the opinion that we will have two more good sugar crops and then the industry will collapse or pay much too little to make it worthwhile. But they offered us 225,000 dollars and I believe it is too little. Now comes that phase, so entertaining, of haggling over prices; of entering the big shot's office asking for more and then

1. Marius Bewley, 'The Poetry of Wallace Stevens," *Partisan Review* 16 (September 1949): 895–915.
2. Published by Ediciones Orígenes.

after salutations mandarinesques, leaving the fat man with the pen-
cil and the paper inscribed in figures in the hand. It will go on and
on. But I am certain I will get what I want.

I am searching through my books but I do not find "A Primitive
Like an Orb." Where can I obtain the pamphlet?[3]

The season here is very gay: Heifetz, Rodzinski, Rubinstein. And
a so-so Spanish company which presented Benavente and Calderon's
"Life is a Dream." The theatre is a fine show but only when the actors are first class. This Spanish company which has the audacity to
call themselves Compañia Lope de Vega is not what we expected
after all the propaganda from the mother country.

Mariano is exhibiting next Thursday after many years of retire-
ment. He is sending you the catalog of the show. It will be the "exhibition of the year". He is doing some very strange paintings now.
All very somber and abstract, on native themes, like the nañigo
devils who officiate in the negro rituals of the religious order of the
nañigos. He has given up pineapples for the devils.

I want to be in N.Y. for January. I have tickets for *Death of a
Salesman.* So perhaps we shall dine together soon.

Please write again and do let me know about the "Primitive."

José

[Hartford, Connecticut]
December 5, 1949

Dear José:

If you come to New York in January, or, for that matter, any
other time, I shall be glad to come down. You speak of having dinner together. More likely it would be lunch because dinner requires
that one should stay over night and finding accommodations in
New York is a bore. It is much pleasanter to go down in the morning and come back in the evening, particularly since I never want
to stay over night, having no interest in "South Pacific" or night
clubs.

As a matter of fact, I am going down tomorrow. On the one or
two occasions each year when I do stay over night the occasion is

3. *A Primitive like an Orb* (New York: Prospero Pamphlet, Gotham
Book Mart, 1948).

the pretext: the actuality is a long list of errands to run and of people to see. I don't care so much about the errands, but, as the isolation of Hartford and winter and being seventy piles up, one does
like to see old friends occasionally, especially while they are still
alive. Most of them are merely inscriptions and memories. One of
the oldest friends I had became fatally ill last summer. I went down
to see him.[1] He understood the situation perfectly and in order to
get away from it talked about politics and sail boats and eccentric
people who live on some of the islands off the New England Coast.
It takes a certain amount not so much of courage but of wisdom to
brush aside the human predicament and to individualize oneself
sufficiently to make a last call of this sort pleasant instead of pathetic and heart-breaking.

Of course, not all of one's friends have as yet been measured for
their shrouds. The only trouble is that with so many errands to do it
is not possible to see people except in the most casual way and then
one is back in the office again writing to José and other creatures of
the rainbow to the south of us.

I am reading at the moment a collection of letters written by
Romain Rolland to one of his friends, Malwida von Meysenbug.
This was published last year, I believe, by Albin Michel of Paris.[2] I
don't know what your facilities for picking up French books are in
Havana, but I am finding these letters interesting beyond belief and
for no particular reason. Last night one of his letters was full of
complaints about a noisy neighbor. Somehow it interested me immensely to know that one has noisy neighbors in Paris. Rolland, apparently, lived in an apartment where his wife, Clothilde, was no

1. Stevens had traveled to Montclair, New Jersey, to visit Edward B.
Southworth, Jr., one of his oldest friends in the insurance business, on
Saturday, 18 June. Letter from Southworth to Stevens, 23 June 1949,
Huntington Library; the date of the visit is confirmed in *L,* 638. When
Stevens entered the surety business in 1908, joining the New York office
of the American Bonding Company, Southworth was a vice president of
that branch office. Six years later, when Southworth became manager of
the Equitable's New York branch, Stevens was hired there and for two
years Southworth was his boss. Southworth was eighty-one when he died
on 16 September 1949.
2. Romain Rolland, *Choix de Lettres à Malwida Meysenbug* (Paris:
Albin Michel, 1948).

more hostile to a little dust than we are at home but the neighbors seemed to have moved the chairs every Thursday and cleaned the windows every Friday, polished the kitchen floor every Saturday, did the laundry on Sunday, dusted on Monday, etc. Rolland thought that this was the last word in being bourgeois. How much more closely that sort of thing brings one to Paris than remarks about the growth of interest in Socialism, the artificiality of Sarah Bernhardt, the facility with which Duse was able to weep on the stage, the slightly ironic sneer that D'Annunzio always wore. I like, too, as typical of what interests me in the book, his praises of the nobility of Rome as compared to the ennui of Paris, but of course Paris was full of ennui for him because it was there that he worked and met people that he did not like. In Rome he nourished his sense of nobility and met only people that he liked.

As a matter of fact, I started this very largely to wish you a Merry Christmas and a Happy New Year and I do, I do, I do.

Always sincerely yours,
Wallace Stevens

[Hartford, Connecticut]
January 26, 1950

Dear José:

I have been wanting for some time to write to you to say how much I enjoyed the Felicidades which you and Mari[an]o were cheerful enough to send me at the end of the year. But so many things have happened since then that I have not been able to get around to it. Also I had in the back of my mind the possibility that you might be coming to New York and that I should be seeing you. This possibility will no doubt sooner or later be realized. I have little more than that on my mind at the moment. I do not want either you or Mari[an]o, whom I do not as yet have the pleasure of knowing, to think that I was indifferent to what really gave me a great deal of pleasure.

I have not been to New York since last month. There are a lot of things that are of interest. There is the statue loaned by the Italian government which is on exhibition at the Metropolitan and which is as important as anything else. Then, too, there is quite a show at

Wildenstein's; not to speak of Eliot's play.[1] It would do me good to go down for a week, walk around, go to concerts and theatres and meet a few pleasant people. But this is one of the busiest times of our year here. The drawback is that with all there is to do there is so much bad weather: I mean mist and rain. When the sun shines it is as gorgeous as it is in Cuba. But it seems to shine only one or two days a week.

Greetings and best wishes and with every hope of being able to see you again, I am

Very truly yours,
Wallace Stevens

La Habana, Cuba
Jan.–Feb. 23, 1950

My dear Wallachio:

Excuse this prolonged silence. I haven't been well. I had just been operated in the throat. And now I am getting ready for the appendicitis operation. So if I see you in March (as I hope), I shall be a "new" man. Even the tone of my voice will be new, fresh.

I finally sent for a "Primitive" the poem I asked you about. Gotham Book Mart will send it along soon.

I also sent for a ticket for *The Cocktail Party* which I saw advertised in a *New Yorker* here. So you see I am planning an escape very, very soon, my dear friend. And yet I am very contented here; I am pondering seriously the idea of forgetting the *claustros* of Princeton or Harvard and settling down again in *la bella Havana*. The days are very magnificent now, in January, and it's a pleasure to go to the beaches and assume the horizontal and watch the sea blue and quiet and look at seagulls maneuvering about for—a fish! Just that; no more; no less.

I heard from Miss M. Moore. She tells me her mother died. She

1. In late December and early January, a special exhibit of Persian art, on loan from the Iranian government, appeared at the Metropolitan Museum. An exhibit of Rembrandts to benefit the Public Education Association appeared at Wildenstein's Gallery on 64th Street, opening the week of 21 January. Eliot's *Cocktail Party,* starring Alec Guinness, appeared at the Henry Miller Theatre.

must be awfully lonely in her Brooklynese Apt. with no one to look
after, but the gray cat and the faded geraniums. I have been re-reading Nietzsche and the *Bros. Karamazov*. I was put to it by a recent
perusal of Chestov's *The Philosophy of Tragedy*.[1] I was amazed to
discover how much I like *now* these two great "moles" or men-
from-the-underground. It's not that they bring a formula to make
accessible or justifiable my egotism. Simply, they did *dare* to look at
life in the face and to see that it was a tragic and awful thing. Well,
of course, it's a matter of temperament. But I enjoy their vision of
"things" human.

Feb. 1950

Since I was writing to you about Chestov, life has become quite
complicated. I had an attack of appendicitis and last week had the
appendix removed, "extirpated," as my doctor (who likes Matisse)
likes to explain. I feel now younger and lighter. I am looking forward to my escape to N.Y. City. I have received the ticket to Eliot's
comedy. I expect to be in Princeton around the 25th of March.

I am recuperating quite successfully. Here I am, sitting by my sister Olga's piano; she is playing Turina's "Scaro-Monte"; there is a
nice breeze blowing and the flowers giving the lie to all the news
from the U.S. saying that the world up there is frozen to the roots. I
really feel sorry for you, up in coldish Hartford. But then, you are
probably more actively "engaged" in life and literature. I am getting lazier. I'd rather walk by the sea; look about at people and
scenery than put pen to papers.

I have been reading Gilbert Sitwell's short stories—*Triple
Fugue*[2]—which I find charming, baroque evocations of things very
English and very pastel in their colours—from this vantage point,
geographic and timely. He seems like a very rare bird, a tropical,
splendorous bird, amid the quite anemic, pale, dolorous-looking literary crowd which surges from the British scene. I don't know if
you like Edith. She doesn't excite me too much. But they are quite
a refreshing change from Isherwood, Spender, G[raham] Green,

1. Leon Chestov (Lev Shestov), *La philosophie de la tragedie: Dos-
toiewsky et Nietzsch* (Paris: J. Schiffrin, 1929).
2. José mistakes Gilbert for Osbert Sitwell, *Triple Fugue* (New York:
G. H. Doran, 1925).

and other English jugglers. Joyce Cary's novels are up in turn. I like her (or his?) *Horse's Mouth* which is quite funny (up to page 101). What have you read or heard about, worthy of my consideration? Did you look up K[enneth] Burke's amazing piece in *Sewanee* on Roethke's vegetal poetry?[3] And *P[artisan] R[eview]*'s symposium on Religion and the Intellectuals (Bosh!).[4] I recommend Borges' "The Zahir" in that issue (Feb.)[5] He is one of the most brilliant and queerest writers down Argentina way. I like his poetry best; his prose is splendid, his essays are ruthless denigrations of the false little gods the Argentines like to set up as crutches to their vanity. Enfin, everyone is invidious of his great talent but no one can quite imitate or do better than he.

Mariano is in Camagüery exhibiting his pictures; hoping furiously to convert our guajíros to his modern style. Did you see in *Orígenes* the reproductions of his last work?

How is your friend in Ceylon? I hope he has begun to put your poetry into his beautiful language.

I am a little tired, so I will put an end to this rather chaotic communication. I hope you are not too cold and I still want you to transport yourself to this eternal Cuban summer. Our modest house is at your disposal always.

Yours devotedly,
José

[Princeton, New Jersey]
April 21 [1950]

My dear Wallachio:

I have been leading a very quiet simple existence, and I feel it is doing me not a bit of good. I have not returned home, because I feel I should take advantage of this cold weather—as soon as the

3. "The Vegetal Radicalism of Theodore Roethke," *Sewanee Review* 58 (1950): 68–108.

4. "Religion and the Intellectuals, A Symposium: James Agee, Hannah Arendt, Newton Arvin, W. H. Auden, John Dewey, Robert Graves, Marianne Moore, I. A. Richards," *Partisan Review* 17, no. 2 (February 1950): 103–42.

5. Jorge Luis Borges, "The Zahir," translated from the Spanish by Dudley Fitts, *Partisan Review* 17, no. 2 (February 1950): 143–51.

weather gets warmer, I shall pack and return to the green isle. To-night, Lionel Trilling will lecture on Wordsworth whose centenary they are celebrating all over the academic world.

I read a nasty little collection of short stories by a new British writer, Agnes [Angus] Wilson, called *The Wrong Set*.[1] Frankly, they were not as amusing or biting as they had made me believe. I find it more and more difficult to read modern writers. They are on the whole so mediocre. I have been reading also O'Connor's *opus* on Mr. Stevens but it is not *too* stimulating, I must confess.[2]

The spring seems on the verge of bursting forth here. The mag-nolias and the tulips have flowered timidly around the Princeton dormitories. There are some lovely Japanese trees in bloom. The trees are showing a little of their greeness, and the lawns begin to resemble golf courses—so trim, cleaned, well combed. Even the spring behaves around here.

The Freshmen are having a big spring prom. I suppose they are out to welcome the arrival of warm weather, the presence of female companions and sex. Tonight, they will drink, dance, and run around with their girls and feel that everything is fine with this secluded little world of ours.

I have been postponing my trip to Boston until the weather shows some definite constancy. Yesterday it was warm; today it is chilly again. I will let you know when I decide to go north so we can see each other in Hartford, but if you come to N.Y. let me know.

Yours affectionately,
José

[Hartford, Connecticut]
April 24, 1950

Dear José:

Curiously, I was wondering about you yesterday. Princeton, or for that matter, any other place, is at its best in spring. I suppose that you have no spring in Cuba or, if you have, it is not the same

1. London: Secker and Warburg, 1949.
2. *The Shaping Spirit: A Study of Wallace Stevens* (Chicago: Regnery, 1950).

thing as spring up here. I remember thinking that there was no spring in Florida but I found that I was mistaken about that.

The little party that I went to in New York turned out to be unusually agreeable. It was at an apartment a sufficient distance from the center of town to make it possible for one to see the center of town in perspective. It was grandiose in the best sense. The only thing that went wrong was that at about 7 o'clock, when I thought the people might be wanting to have dinner, I asked them what time they were going to have dinner. This brought the house down because they thought that I was asking because I was wondering about my own dinner. As a matter of fact, connections were so close that I went without dinner.

Mr. O'Connor's book has just come in but I have not had a chance to look at it. I expect to find it rather good because he is intelligent and hard-working and, I believe, friendly enough, since otherwise he would not have interested himself in writing the thing. He succeeds a man who had made a most elaborate study of everything and who died, unhappily, before he got around to doing his book, which, for him, would have been his principal book.[1] With Mr. O'Connor this is probably not much more than just a book by a youngish critic looking around for a subject not too hackneyed. Yet I am very much pleased to have had O'Connor do the job. The great danger with all such books is that it makes one self-conscious to read them. If the author types well, there is a disposition to act up to the type, which is a mistake. It would be a complete fraud oneself to do such a thing. Perhaps I shall not read the book too carefully out of fear of just this.

I look forward to a visit from you here one of these days. Spring is the poorest season of the year in New England unless you like a cold, damp spring. Sometimes we have a few marvelous weeks but generally the weather never settles down until about the beginning of July. But come regardless of the weather.

Sincerely,

Wallace Stevens

1. Hi Simons of Chicago had begun working on a checklist of Stevens' poetry in 1935. When he died suddenly ten years later, on 4 April 1945, he had published two essays on Stevens, but he had admitted to Stevens that his "life's work" remained unfinished.

Playa de Guanabo
June 17, 1950

My dear Wallachio:

So many things have kept me in a turmoil that I have not been able to write you since I arrived in Habana. Mostly, family affairs: the sale of two large fincas. The feuds and scramble for the money was something as sordid and disagreeable as those scenes in Mauriac's novels. I was however amused by the whole comedy—I took it philosophically. I was only after mother's share, $200,000. Now, I am going to build a large apt. house and on the top floor shall have my pent-house. Because mother's business affairs need an overseer, I have decided not to return to Princeton. So I shall live here until next April when mother, Olga and I shall leave for Spain.

I hope you are spending a delightful summer. Here in Guanabo Beach—an hour by car from town—we have rented a lovely house for the summer—facing a wonderful blue Caribbean sea—and I read and write and rest contented. Last night, I was sitting in the porch—there was a sweet breeze blowing (no bitter winter wind here) and the sky full of stars—and I was wondering why you don't retire and come down to these tropical lands you admire so and just rest among these glittering surroundings. I shall send you some pictures of the house and beach as soon as they are developed.

At the moment, I am reading *Art as Expression* [*Experience*] of John Dewey in a Spanish translation[1] and the poems of Luis Cernuda, a very fine poet, an exile who teaches at Mt. Holyoke.[2] By the way, he told me you had been there to give a lecture last year. My, but you move about!

How is the *Auroras del Otoño* coming? I am looking forward to its publication. José Lezama thought the title very Stevensiano. He admires you very much—ever since he read your poem about Habana in *Avarice*.[3]

1. *El arte como experiencia* (Mexico: Fondo de Cultura Economica, 1949).

2. Cernuda left Spain after the civil war, taught at the universities of Glasgow, Cambridge, and London, and was in his third year of a four-year term at Mount Holyoke. Stevens had given the Kimball lecture at Mount Holyoke two years earlier, on 2 April 1948. The college later awarded Stevens an honorary doctorate.

3. "Academic Discourse at Havana" appeared in *Revista de avance.*

Well, my dear Wallachio, I hope you are having a happy summer in far-away New England. Please remember that if I don't put pen to paper, I think often of you and keep wishing you would come down to visit us.

Yours affectionately,
José

[Hartford, Connecticut]
August 15, 1950

Dear José:

I have asked Knopf, the publisher, to send you a copy of *The Auroras of Autumn* and he now says that he has done so. A little later on, when I have received more copies than I need right now, I shall send one to your friend [Lezama] Lima. The book is very well done: well printed and well got up. Parts of one of your letters to me appear in one of the poems: "The Novel." This same poem includes a quotation from Lorca which I picked up in a letter to me from a friend in Dublin, Tom McGreevy, who also appears in the book. He is now director of the Irish National Gallery.

Weren't you going to send me snapshots of the earthly paradise you inhabit? Where are they? I need some such thing in the dead center of summer and not a particularly pleasant summer either meteorologically or otherwise, except in Korea where it is possible to shoot Communists. Yet I continue to receive occasional messages from Europe which indicate that the mania of Marxism has not yet seized the whole world. Weather or no weather, people still lunch on the terraces of Paris and drink Chablis; and they still travel in Spain; and the lakes of Switzerland are still blue and the little steamers on them toot-toot-toot (in Swiss).

Literature, that great affaire of yours, is rather dull. I have read Jean Paulhan's *Causes Celebres*[1] with care appropriate to Paulhan, who thinks about everything yet is never inspired. He is, after all, intellectual without emotion. But he is a delicious workman, if I may say such a thing. At the moment I am reading a Penguin Classic, [E. V.] Rieu's translation of *Iliad*. I have just sent for several

---

1. Paris: Gallimard, 1950.

books by Henri Pourrat. Pourrat is a curé of a French village in
Auvergne. He and Henry Church were great friends and that is how
I know of him. He is a marvelous story teller. While he is just as
sophisticated as Paulhan, nevertheless he loves people: his own con-
gregation and, I suppose, everyone else around him, so much more
than Paulhan really loves anybody. He is a great find. I love the
sense of reading an exquisite man whom very few people know
anything about and with whom there are no vulgarizations whatever
associated. In addition to writing and doing his job as a priest,
Pourrat manufactures paper, the kind of paper on which one would
like to print one or two poems. And I believe that he does other
things besides.[2]

I have not been to New York since June. The exhibition of
[Edvard] Munch in the Museum of Modern Art almost persuaded
me to take the trouble to go down. However, he is a repulsive
painter. Perhaps there are varieties of repulsiveness. The repulsiveness of a wild northerner dying of tuberculosis is the particular
variety in which Munch engaged although I believe he did not die
of tuberculosis. There are Swedish paintings in which the color will
tell you that the painter was at the point of death from pernicious
anemia and there are Norwegian dramas which tell you that the
dramatist was a poisoner and assassin. Munch lived in that sort of a
world: the world of cancer, poverty. I imagine that his exhibition
must have been a great success because in a world like the world
of New York Munch would be something violently new and, say,
almost criminally unpleasant.

Adieu. Write to me when you can.

Sincerely,
Wallace Stevens

2. Through their correspondence, Henry Church introduced Stevens to
Henri Pourrat; Church later enlisted Stevens' aid in his attempt to raise
interest in publishing Pourrat's work in America. Pourrat edited *Hommage
à Henry Church* (Paris: Mesures, 1948), which Stevens praised; see *L,*
591. Stevens later ordered two of Pourrat's works, *Le Sage et son démon*
(Paris: Albin Michel, 1950) and *Contes de la bucheronne* (Tours: Maison
Mame, 1936).

Habana, Cuba
October the 3rd [1950]

My dear Mr. Stevens:

Sorry to have prolonged this reply to your very wonderful present. The *Auroras* came in double gifts: I have already given Lezama Lima his copy. He shall write you, but wants me to thank you once more for your very thoughtful action. I found the book magnificent; it is quite incredible how your poetry becomes sharper, younger, more exhilarating with the passing of time. A group of *Orígenes* readers and colaborators came to my house the other night, and I tried to put across to them the lovely texture and resonance of some of your poems. How wonderfully they understood poems like "The Owl in the Sarcophagus" and the New Haven poem. I translated some, like "The Novel" and the "Auroras", as best I could. A bit of an improvisation, but they were all delighted. I am quite a translator if I may say so. Thank you again.

I didn't write, because I have been away at Guanabo and returned a few days ago. Then I read your letter and went to pick up the books. I had a very nice summer; if you see me now you would probably think me a mestizo—so darkly bronzed I have become. At the present moment, I am very busy on the construction of an apartment house for mother which will cost around $200,000 in the Vedado, and I am taking all the construction details into my hands. So I am running back and forth getting cement here, steel there, etc. I believe I shall become quite a businessman in time. Very little reading: Maurois' *Proust*,[1] some Spanish novels and poetry. I have translated H. James' *Balzac* for *Orígenes* since this is the Centenary of his death. It is the second essay he wrote on the grand old man and it is a lulu. The most difficult piece of Anglish prose I have tackled. It was a piece "bristling with difficulties" as James would put it.

I hope the auroras continue to visit you now that the fall is descending over Hartford. I hope to write you soon and speak of more personal matters. There has come quite a transformation

1. José was probably reading André Maurois' *A la recherche de Marcel Proust* (Paris: Hatchett, 1949) or *Proust: Portrait of a Genius* (New York: Harper, 1950).

in the glass house. Once more from Lezama and I, muchas gracias.

José

Jan. 3 [1951]

My dear Wallachio:

I was delighted to see your kind message; always remembrances from Hartford, a luminosity of your own which suffuses your good words of felicitation as well as the more genial aspects of your poesía. I have been recovering from a long illness here, in the clinic Miramar, when the tall negro boy—a messenger from Almendares—introduced his skinny, black fingers into the room, in his hand like a white bird of good omens and warm news—your letter! I was sad on reading your message—remembering, dear friend, how I have neglected you over these past months. Really, life has been a turmoil over the past months. Mother very excited. Finally, she became ill and is now in the Sanatorium in Guanabacoa, across the Bay of Habana. She had been well for the last two years and a half. So I was apprehensive; however, she was soon to become nervous once more. It is a terrible cross we bear, who have to live in the company of someone with a mental illness. But then there is no one I love and care more for than her and wouldn't change my existence for anyone else.

After her illness, I came down with this intestinal affliction: the pancreas was not functioning well. And so I have been here for two weeks now. I thought, however, what great consolation!, to find myself suffering of the pancreas—a strange, seldom named organ with such an exotic name. I can imagine a phrase like *Las Islas Pancreáticas, The Planet Pancreas,* or *"Demetrius Pancreas,* a genius for mystification, came in with a strange tie. His smile told us, sitting under the Aegean sun, that nothing good would come from having dispersed the flock of goats"* (beginning of some banal novelette). Well, the pancreas is behaving much better, and I think I shall return home tomorrow.

Now that mother is ill and away, I'll probably go to the sugar mill and spend a month there, smelling the sweet breezes and hearing the "twangling noises" of the big grinders. Last year we made a hell of a lot of money and this year the crop will probably be even better.

I am reading a great amount. Just finished a very amusing novel, *Cefalû* by the English poet (?) Lawrence Durrell.[1] I haven't received a magazine in the last 4 months. If you have around *The New Statesman, Hudson, Kenyon* or any other little reviews and if you are going to drop them into your basket, don't! Send them to me. The same with European reviews. Habana is every day less sophisticated in these matters; impossible to find anything worth while to read outside of Hemingway's detestable new novel. Now "Ernie" is entertaining Gary Cooper who said on arriving: "Cuba is just what I dreamed it was" etc.[2]

I am sending you the last *Orígenes,* just out. I have there inserted my translation of H[enry] James' essay on *Balzac:* his second devotional "homage" to the great master (1914). Has anything exciting occurred in the American lit. scene these past six months?

I don't know when I shall be able to return North. As I wrote, I am in charge of the construction of the apartment House for mother which is going up in the Vedado, and will probably be busy with masons, carpenters, electricians until the summer.

Habana is just as marvelous as ever. Now Josephine Baker is here. She is *wonderful* at 53. All "habaneros" have taken her to heart. Last night she entertained at a big party given by a Cuban sugar man—*Aspirin*—and was heard to exclaim, "Never have I seen such display of wealth, beauty and champagne!"[3] She came for a week; that was four weeks ago. That goes to show how the Cubans can take by storm even the most Parisian, sophisticated, and mundane of the world's vedettes.[4]

1. London: Poetry, 1947.
2. Winter 1950–51 brought to Hemingway's villa a constant flow of visitors, including Cooper, Tom Shevlin, Winston Guest, and Patricia Neal. The "detestable new novel" was *Across the River and into the Trees* (New York: Scribner's, 1950).
3. Is José remembering and paying tribute to the Canon Aspirin of Stevens' "Notes toward a Supreme Fiction" and perhaps alluding to the relish with which Aspirin and his guests enjoyed "lobster Bombay with mango/Chutney"? (*CP,* 401).
4. Josephine Baker (1906–74), American-born French singer of revues and operettas at the Folies Bergères.

As a matter of fact, reading the paper tonight I felt a little sad. Why don't we "cubanize" a little the world? Then everybody would take it easier, would live for today, leave things for *mañana,* and get along better with their neighbors. I see N.Y. is ready for an atomic attack. From here, my dear friend, everything you read sounds a bit fantastical and absurd. Maybe we are (the Spaniards and Cubans) a race of retarded mortals. We still live by norms of other centuries and will not recognize completely the mechanical urge. Just to prove this point: in Habana the new *cafetera* (little engine that makes coffee) are called (as advertisement) *La Bomba Atómica.* That sense of humour has saved us from the madness and nonsense that threatens to end your more "civilized" histories.

The nurse is back. I must lie down to rest (not to die). I hope your "paladar" will taste new things, and your poetry will continue to shine brighter and brighter in this 1951.

I am as ever your devoted,
José

P.S. I am still dreaming with your visit. All Cuba will make you happy and warm.

VIES IMAGINAIRES

1951–1955

Three days into the year 1951 José had
been dreaming, as he had written, of Stevens' visit to Cuba. But not
only did Stevens not visit him; he did not write. It was their longest
silence. José sent Christmas greetings in December, but when Stevens wrote back three days before the end of the year, his tone had
changed. He seemed older still. He seemed to José to be more disso-
ciated from the people immediately around him and even from his
culture. When he closed the door to his room on Christmas Day, he
wrote that he "felt as if [he] was shutting out something crude and
lacking in all feeling and delicacy." As if shocked by this admission,
he quickly corrects himself: "Of course I am completely wrong."
When Stevens agreed to purchase yet another book suggested by
José's card, he hardly knew how this book, *Vies Imaginaires* by
Marcel Schwob, would give José the opportunity to criticize him
harshly for his tendency to correct himself after making an honest
statement about his isolation. José also took the opportunity to
clarify the difference in how each man viewed the connection between literature and life.

Stevens purchased a copy of *Vies Imaginaires* in New York on
Saturday, 29 December 1951, at the French Book Shop, and wrote
José in January dismissing Schwob out of hand. In his long response of 25 February, José's rigorous distinction between Schwob
and André Gide leads him to imply strongly that a similar distinction holds between himself and Stevens respectively. He wasn't fully

aware of the extent to which Stevens had always favored Gide's moral strength, but in this letter he makes it clear that what Stevens would call Schwob's weakness was more sincere than Gide's so-called toughness. José liked Schwob's acquiescence to the pain of loneliness and illness, the *esthétique du mal,* and despised Gide's emphasis on duty and will. José appreciated Schwob's celebration of the wandering, adventuresome ego (Schwob was a neoromantic but had learned from the realists, loved Stevenson's novels, and theorized on the *roman d'aventure*) while disparaging Gide's "monstrous mystification of the ego" and the way his journeys are motivated by personal and intellectual indecision. He liked Schwob's ornamentation and had grown impatient with Gide's puritan journalism. In an attempt to appeal to Stevens' love of the indigenous, José notes how horrified Gide was by something as native to southern culture as the blood of the bullfighter. José's thesis about Gide, which he had elaborated in an essay entitled "André Gide, Icarus without a Sun," written a year earlier for *Orígenes,* was that Gide should be considered in the literary tradition of puritanism, that it helps when placing his work to "remember that he was not a Catholic." José wrote, "In this sense, Gide is precursor—supreme irony—of contemporary North American literature." When reminded recently of this obvious assault on Stevens' own literary tradition, José said, "Gide is Protestant. I don't think Stevens understood that point."

Stevens had been collecting the volumes of Gide's *Journal,* and also bought a copy of *Robert* (1930) from the bookshop where later he found Schwob. By 1947 Stevens had formed his favorable opinion of Gide's toughness; it comforted him that in "this present time of skepticism . . . and nihilism," Gide promoted the redemption of an individual spirit through work (*L,* 601). From previous complaints Stevens has made about José—one who "looks too deeply to see the bottom of things" in contrast to the señora who knows cows and chickens—readers can perhaps predict Stevens' determination to let Gide serve as a positive model. To Stevens, writing in 1950 after having read the letters between Gide and Paul-Louis Claudel, Gide's toughness constituted an ability to go untrapped "in a world of traps" (*L,* 670).

José disagreed intensely about the value of Gide's writing (he called *The Immoralist* "a very mediocre work"), but there is more than literature at stake when he makes the distinction between Gide and Schwob in the polemic of this critical letter. Gide's (and Stevens') tentativeness, being tantamount to insincerity, indicated an unlived life made still less redeemable by moralism: "I prefer Schwob's pure ornamentation to Gide's 'pure' sincerity . . . Gide's struggles seem a bore. . . . But remember," he adds with determined irony, "Gide's search for a climate!"

Gide had defected from the influence of Oscar Wilde, José notes in his essay, in the manner in which an intellectual man "nostalgic for his ordering thought" defects from a "great singer of male beauty." In short, Gide had abandoned conviction and sensuality for "his good philosophy of language." Here is the heart of the matter between Stevens and José: José denigrates those who believe that art provides us with a philosophy of language and thereby a philosophy of life. But in order to do so he must suggest that a man like Oscar Wilde comes down hard on the side of life and against language, a suggestion, whether true or false, that Stevens would not have accepted.

In 1952, as each argued that the other preferred literature to life, José's friend Lezama Lima celebrated *Orígenes* in the retrospective essay "Signs," in which he summarized the Orígenes Group as having continually defined the fashionable dualism that was keeping life and books apart—in "literalizing life and living literature," as he put it. *Orígenes* had been designed to work against those who criticized a book for being "pure literature," as Stevens did Schwob's book.

Would it be as plain to Stevens as it was now to José that the problem with Gide was Stevens' problem? José wrote of Gide that he "cannot forge for himself an image of his life which is very . . . convincing. . . . In vain he would move between the two dilemmas of existence and of thought; of looking and not sharing in the life that surrounded him, so full of temptation and delights." Only occasionally had Stevens shown he understood this essential aspect of himself.

[Hartford, Connecticut]
December 27, 1951

Dear José:

I had you in mind shortly before Christmas but I intended to write to you because I owed you a letter. But that intention, like a good many others, came to nothing. I did not even send Christmas cards except to one or two people with whom I am closely associated. I think that if people took advantage of this time to renew friendships, write letters, make visits, etc., it would really be a precious holiday. Actually, we have people who seem to hand a list of names to a stenographer and tell her to shoot the works. I shrink from all that. We stayed at home. My daughter and her little boy came on Christmas afternoon and we had a very pleasant dinner after which she went home to do a little large-scale entertaining on her own account. My wife and I were ready to go upstairs at seven o'clock. When I went up and closed the door of my room I felt as if I was shutting out something crude and lacking in all feeling and delicacy. Of course I am completely wrong, but, nevertheless, that was my real sensation. Thank goodness it is over.

I cannot tell you how agreeable it is to have your letter. For the last three or four months I have hardly had time to read a line. Now your letter reminds me of Marcel Schwob who is somebody or other's son-in-law and whose work I know in a sort of way. I shall try to pick up *Vies Imaginaires* in New York where I am going the day after tomorrow to attend a meeting of the judges who will award the National Book Award for 1951. I shall have only a few hours there and expect to see no one. But I have a number of other books that I want to pick up, among them, possibly, a little set of Chaucer if I am able to find a set without more notes than text. Last summer, or was it the summer before, they held a sort of seminar at Harvard for the benefit, no doubt, of the Summer School. The subject was the defense of poetry. They were kind enough to send me a transcript of the minutes and I spent two solid days reading this transcript over the holiday without getting very much of anything out of it in which I believed, except the idea that I might enjoy Chaucer's "Troilus and Cressida". I assume that in order to read this single poem I shall have to buy five volumes of Chaucer.

I am writing today because I want to wish you a happy New

Year. It gives me the greatest pleasure to hear from you and, as you know, to find things in your letter about your family and friends because these things really add something to life whereas most ideas don't, and most people want to write to me about ideas.

I shall write to you soon again. In the meantime, and always, with my very best wishes, I am

Sincerely yours,
Wallace Stevens

Habana, Cuba
February 22 [1952]

My dear Wallachio:

I have translated your fine essay on "The Relations between Poetry and Painting." The reason I would prefer to publish this essay to "Imagination as Value," which I have already put into Spanish, is due to Mariano's great interest in what you have to say there about his own art. *Orígenes* is ready to go to the printer's; so if we can have the honour and privilege of publishing your essay I would like you to let me know as soon as possible.[1] There is a word "ambiance" on page 174, fourth line from the bottom which I presume means *environment:* does it? I could not find it in my Webster.

It was very strange: when I read about Villon. I had beside me the last *Cahiers d'Art* where there is an essay on his works, with profuse illustrations. In that same issue, there are reproductions of our fine Cuban painter, Wilfredo Lam, and an essay on Picasso's etchings by María Zambrano, a disciple of Ortega y Gasset, who has been living in Cuba the last 6 years. Perhaps, you have seen other essays of María in *Orígenes.*

Today we had a nice shooting feud in Prado Street between a

1. José's translation of Stevens' essay appeared in *Orígenes* 9, no. 30 (1952): 34–42. The paper had been read at the Museum of Modern Art on 15 January 1951 and was published by the museum as a pamphlet. Mariano was not the only one of the *origenistas* interested in the connections between poetry and painting. José himself had recently translated an essay on Braque and edited a collection of aphoristic phrases by the painter: *Orígenes* 8, no. 28 (1951): 5–10.

Police Sargeant and two Habana gangsters. One of them [?] nick-named "Pistolita" (little pistol) was severely wounded; a passer-by named Madariaga—no relation of Salvador—was killed. He was on his way to buy a ticket for Venezuela; instead he purchased a one-way passage to Heaven.[2] The street (Prado) was filled with tourists from the ship Italia (!) which came in on a cruise. So your fellow country-men got a good *dosis* of Latin excitement; shooting, blood running among greenest boughs, and the strange sight of Negro boys screaming (while the bullets whizzed by their exotically-adorned heads) *"Maracas, maracas!,* buy a Cuban maraca!" I saw the whole show, because I was across the street buying a painting for my apartment. So you see, the search for experience still has its recompenses, if *you visit Cuba in the winter.* Another street scene I beheld this morning: two ragamuffins yelling at the top of their voices: "Mister, a dollar please!" (This is quite funny, because they usually yell a "penny, mister".) The American couple were amazed, but one of the little Negro boys explained quickly: "The cost of living has gone up, lady" in perfect American lingo.

—Late Evening

I am reading *Life.* C'est la vie! I saw our admired M. Moore getting her award for her book of *Collected Poetry.*[3] "It is hard to think of a thing more out of time than nobility," W. Stevens.

Lezama Lima tells me you sent Lorenzo García Vega a very lovely note thanking him for his book *Espirales Del Cuje,*[4] a won-derful and poetic description of a *criollo* world which is fastly dis-appearing from among us. Those fine gestures on your part are what has converted you, my dear Wallachio, to an almost legendary amigo of us Cuban writers. Partly, because I believe the real cause lies in your poetry where our poets discern a certain colour, a cer-

2. As the *New York Times* reported the event, the gangsters were "rev-olutionaries" and the police sergeant was protecting a member of the Cuban House of Representatives whose life had been threatened by assassins.

3. The "People" section of the 11 February 1952 issue of *Life* included a photograph of Marianne Moore seated with James Jones and Rachel Carson, all of whom received National Book Awards in 1951.

4. Havana: Ediciones Orígenes, 1951.

tain light—a beauty—which so very much evokes our own delicate
paysage. I have often invited you to come and pay us a visit. I hope
soon you will be able to visit us.

As I told you in my last letter, I'll probably go to Europe this
spring. If I go via N. York I will surely call you up. But write soon
and tell me about your doings.

Yours affectionately,
Pepe

[Hartford, Connecticut]
February 19, 1952

Dear José:

About "Imagination as Value": I wrote to Mr. Knopf's office
and enclose the reply. Whatever you have to pay, I shall be glad to
pay back to you. This sort of thing is something that I cannot avoid.
Also, it is something to which in nine cases out of ten I have no
objection, because it puts the thing on a business basis which sim-
plifies it. Let me know what you do pay and, as I say, I shall refund
what you have to pay.

About other things: When your letter came, commiserating in
respect to the weather, there was not a flake of snow on the ground
and we had been having a week or two of peerless days and nights
à la mode de Cartier. Then, suddenly, we had almost a foot of snow.
But it doesn't matter because the worst of winter is over. I have not
been having a particularly good time—not a bad time, but a dull
time, with a lot to do and a loss of interest in things in general. For
example, I found a copy of the little book by Marcel Schwob of
which you spoke and after reading thirty or forty pages put it down
with a feeling that it was definitely effete. My interest is not in pure
literature of that type.

Tomorrow I am going to New York to do a number of errands
and otherwise nothing at all. Perhaps I shall have my hair cut. I
know almost no one there any more, so that I am like a ghost in a
cemetery reading epitaphs. I am going to visit a bookbinder, a dealer
in autographs, Brooks about pajamas, try to find a copy of *Revue
de Paris* for December because of an article about Alain[1] that it

1. Henri Mondor's "Alain," pp. 5–16.

contains, visit a baker, a fruit dealer and, as it may be, a barber. An ordinary day like that does more for me than an extraordinary day: the bread of life is better than any souffle. I have joined a club down there in order to rescue a place from the placeless. Thus it is now possible for me to knock about and then have somewhere to go without having to buy a brandy and soda, which, in any event, I would never buy anywhere.

I suppose the coming on of spring has much to do with this state of mind. It is almost as if everything was going to be all right again—as if the boards were to be taken down, the windows washed, fresh curtains put up, all on account of the arrival of a rich aunt who before she leaves will whisper in my ear that she intends to leave everything to me, including her chic little villa in Almendares, next door to the blackest eyes in Cuba. Ah! Mon Dieu, how nice it is to drop fifty years in the wastebasket. It is the same thing as writing a poem all night long and then finding in the morning that it is so much the best thing that one has ever done—something to make them ring the chimes.

Of course, I do not forget how deeply you are set in literature and how certain all its excitements have you in its grasp. I have sent to England for a series of little books on modern European writers to be published in the spring. Countess Nelly de Vogüé[2] is coming to New York to promote a new review and I hope to see her. She lives in the Rue Vaneau where Gide lived. I associate the name of de Vogüé either with the *Revue des Deux Mondes* or with a moderately good Burgundy. "Colonnade" is to be revived in London.[3] Marianne Moore is going to spend the summer in France, and so on. Pfui! c'est lá, la literature moderne, n'est-ce pas?

Sincerely yours,
Wallace Stevens

2. Nelly du Vogüé and Stevens had corresponded about her plans to establish *La Revue Libre*. See *L*, 744.

3. *The Colonnade* was a review of belle lettres published by the Andiron Club of New York between 1914 and 1922.

[Havana]
25 *de Febrero-azul—*
calientico [1952]

My dear Primitive:

Last night I walked over to Calle Enamorados; a lovely name for
a street, but quite empty of *enamorados*—saw only two gray cats
who had a starving look in their empty eyes—and posted your letter.
This morning from la Cabaña Fortress across the bahia de la Habana
guns sounded off to greet the International American Defense Junta
which has come down to get a sun-tan and hear the bongos play;
meanwhile they will pretend they need a few naval bases and air
bases "just in case, you know"; the morning was very clear and cool;
the temperature has gone up now (12:15 p.m.); anyways I was
reading about the Aga Khan[1] and his heart collapse—a collapse in
diamonds if the poor Khan can't survive this affliction—when
mother came in with a letter, an inquisitive look: "Did you have an
accident or something": I guess she had seen Accident in your envelope and had come to some tragic conclusions—all by herself. By
your message I gather you had a dull winter; how is that possible?
Some day someone must write an opus on the effects of climate on
the imagination. To my tropical imagination, for instance, Monsieur
Schwob doesn't appear effete at all; I would call his sketches imag-
inary nonsense: a bit of Gallic humor and Semite love for the
archaeological bringing us a diverting piece of souffle, e.g. the last
vie. But at times that sort of literature has its moments of delight. I
suppose you mean by "effete" his polished prose which certainly is
that and nothing else. Like Mr. Pater. But then Mr. Gide's *Voyage
d'Urien* is effete too; although it has its darker insinuations for an
eye more perceiving. Monsieur Schwob married the Spanish actress
Margerita Moreno, who devotedly took care of him in his last years
of an atrocious illness. Monsieur Gide is another story—remember
his: "It is a duty to make oneself happy" or "I need to learn all over
again, and methodically, how to be happy," "It's painful for me to
be happy"—then he writes elsewhere in that monstrous mystification
of the Ego: "I have found the secret of my boredom in Rome; I do
not find myself interesting here." How Puritan Mr. Gide! Exception

1. The obese leader of Ismaili Moslems.

made of his beautiful prose—not always effete—rather crystal-hard—
and his excruciating search for himself—a bit pathetic like Mr.
Lawrence of Arabia—I can't digest his books. See, for instance, this
bit of Puritan horror about bullfights: "The bull is killed in a state
of mortal sin. He has been forced into that state. He himself only
wanted to graze, etc." Sometimes I get the feeling that that was
Monsieur Gide's only hope: just to graze. He forgets the bullfighter
altogether! That same man so horrified by the *fiesta,* can confess
without shame that he was bored at the Auteuil races (1906) and
"my demoralization came especially from having paced the public
exposure over and over without meeting a single person with whom
I wanted to talk or *go to bed"!!* Didn't he realize that he was in
mortal sin, too, when pacing up and down that horse arena?

All these citations have a point: Mr. Gide's imagination. So if you
read him and Monsieur Schwob you'll see what I am trying to get
at. It's better to have an archaeological imagination than an atrophied imagination. I prefer Schwob's pure ornamentation to Gide's
"pure" sincerity. It's a matter of temperament. To my tropical senses
all of Gide's struggles seem a bore. Why didn't he make up his
mind and go to bed with the grocer boy and stop all that nonsense
about God and the mortal sin? An Antillean goes to bed and that's
that. But remember Gide's search for a climate! That search responded to an atrophied imagination.

You say I am deeply set in literature. But I find no difference
between what I read and what I live. Or let us say that I do not
read in order to find any other values except a little pleasure to turn
about the attention of the Imaginative eye. I think a man from your
latitude has other intentions when he picks up a book. But then
your intentions are all quite different from ours. Perhaps, we are
more superficial and frivolous about the arts than the Nordic men.
Mr. Ortega y Gasset would certainly subscribe to that last state of
affairs.

To jump to more ordinary and pleasant subjects: my dog Linda
disappeared many years ago—well, two years ago. Remember?
Well, mother has found another Linda. This is a Dalmatian puppy,
quite pretty. The only trouble: she likes rose petals and whenever
any of these rose plants flower, there she is—Linda—chewing away
with the most innocent look in her lovely eyes. Another instance—
if you please—of tropical imagination, in Dalmatia Linda would

have no rose petals to chew on and she would probably spend her days running back and forth after geese or some other poor *avis*. But my Linda has had the fortune of finding herself in a more congenial climate. Here she basks in the sun all the day; has no master to push her after unworthy tasks; and she can just sit and wait until the rose petals bloom again. What felicity! What a happy life Linda leads in this tropical garden of Almendares. Do you think sincerely she would change her lot for that of a Nordic labrador bitch?

Adieu! I am going to visit Mariano and watch how he paints a cock or a red juicy mamey!

Yours devotedly,
José

P.S. I have written Mr. [Herbert] Weinstock for the copyrights—

Hartford, Conn.
June 30, 1952

Dar José:

Greetings! I could not imagine whose writing it was when I saw your envelope this morning.

It is very doubtful whether I shall go down during the period of your visit because next week-end will be a holiday the whole week-end and I suppose that you will be gone by the following one. However, if I should change my mind, I shall let you know.

Curiously, I have been thinking about you and Havana because someone was talking on the radio a day or two ago about trouble with the bus drivers in Havana. They have been wrecking buses in order to procure more pay. It would be much simpler and much more understandable if they took revolvers and shot the people who own the buses or they could stand along the sidewalks and shoot the passengers.

Nothing would be pleasanter than to spend a few hours with you bringing myself up to date.

I have done very little reading—certainly none of importance. The Yale Press is publishing a series of little books about fifty pages long on modern European literary figures.[1] The original edition is printed in England by Bowes and Bowes of Cambridge. The copies

1. The still current series, Yale Studies in English, began in 1898.

that I have read were English copies, one on Rilke by a German, and another on Valery by an English woman. Both were good. But the one on Valery which I read yesterday got mixed up with a lot of Rhine wine that I had for lunch and kept falling out of my hand. When I had finished I thought it was a truly wonderful work and felt relieved that it was over. In any case, I know even less about Valery than I thought I knew. Either one of these books with Rhine wine or Moselle would be hard to improve on.

Why don't you go to Boston and stop over here for lunch some day? Nothing would make me happier than to see you.

Sincerely yours,
Wallace Stevens

Barbizon Plaza Hotel
101 West 58th Street
Central Park South
New York
July 4th [1952]

My dear Wallachio:

Glad to know you like *Orígenes'* presentation of "The Relation Between Poetry and Painting." I notice you have come in for some publicity of late: everywhere I see essays on your work: Martz, Watts, Babette Deutsch, even *Origin* of Massachusetts dedicates an issue to you. There was even an article on the use of the words "nothing" and "nothingness" in your poetry and now they are calling you a philosopher.[1] So how can your vanity be pleased with our little homage, amigo mio?

Am leaving this evening for Habana and I'm truly sorry I could not see you. Probably, I will return in the fall if by then I have rented our new apartment building completely and if mother is well by then. As you know my trip to Europe was postponed because of her illness.

I only did some shopping; saw a few films—one very remarkable and poetic indeed: "Roshomon."[2] I went also to see Brooklyn vs.

1. *Origin* 2, no. 1 (Spring 1952).
2. Kurosawa's award-winning film (1950) reconstructs an eighth-century murder from four different points of view.

Giants several times; found to my dismay you couldn't bet a cent which makes all games so exciting in Habana.

I have been reading *The Need for Roots,* a truly fascinating book by Simone Weil.[3] I wish I could translate a few pages for *Orígenes'* readers. I had the *Rilke* and *Valery* books you recommended sent home to me so I shall read them soon, but I fear the wine will not come with them; perhaps a little café oscuro and $.20 Corona cigar.

Please write soon and if you ever go south let me know. I can't imagine why you have not taken a trip to Cuba or Florida yet.

Yours with affection,
José

[The Christmas card José sent Stevens at the end of 1952 has not been found.]

[Hartford, Connecticut]
January 13, 1953

Dear José:

Your *Alegres Pascuas* greeting was like a wand: a diversion from the normality of the normal. You might think that Christmas in itself would be a diversion. But after seventy-three of them Christmas, too, is part of the normality of the normal. The sudden, sleek sliding of the Rio Yayabo is truly a wand.

Are you visiting some new scene? A young man in a new scene, a new man in a young scene, a young man in a young scene—excuse my guitar. Up here the guitars are stacked along the attic walls for a while.

We have just had a really winter week-end—snow, sleet, rain. I wanted to stay in bed and make for myself a week-end world far more extraordinary than the one that most people make for themselves. But the habitual, customary, has become, at my age, such a pleasure in itself that it is coming to be that that pleasure is at least as great as any. It is a large part of the normality of the normal. And, I suppose, that projecting this idea to its ultimate extension,

---

3. New York: Routledge and Kegan Paul, 1952.

the time will arrive when just to *be* will take in everything without
the least *doing* since even the least doing is irrelevant to pure being.
When the time comes when just to be does in fact take in everything, I may just do my being on the banks of Rio Yayabo.

You will already have observed the abstract state of my mind.
This is in part due to the fact that I have done little or no reading,
little or no writing or walking or thinking. I have not been to New
York. In short, I have been working at the office, nothing else:
complaining a little about it but content, after all, that I have that
solid rock under my feet, and enjoying the routine without minding
too much that I have to pay a respectable part of my income to the
government in order that someone else representing the government
may sit at the Cafe X at Aix or go to lectures at the Sorbonne.

The Democrats, if they are Democrats, have gone to incredible
lengths in introducing their conception of things into American life
and practice; and just to think of things as they were twenty-five
years ago makes one feel like William Cullen Bryant's great, great
grandfather, to use an expression that someone else used not long
ago. Perhaps the only actual piece of bad luck that I have had is to
allow myself to become conscious of my age. A correspondent in
Paris takes a more cheerful attitude and writes:

> "Ne me parlez plus de vieillesse. Le destin des artistes et des
> poètes est précisement de ne pas vieiller."[1]

It is a good deal truer than one thinks that one's age is largely a
matter of paying attention to it or of not paying attention to it. I am
beginning to feel that it is quite necessary no longer to pay any attention to it.

The only news I have is the awarding of the Bollingen prizes.
Last year was not a conspicuously good year for poetry in this country. The most respectable book published was MacLeish's volume
of collected poems.[2] There was a difference of opinion, however,
about the awarding of the prize because while William Carlos
Williams had not published a volume of poetry last year, his posi-

1. "Don't talk to me of old age. The thing about poets and artists is
they never get old." This was in a letter from the daughter of a Paris art
dealer, Paule Vidal, who corresponded with Stevens after the war.
2. Boston: Houghton Mifflin, 1952.

tion is such that there is a feeling that he ought to have a prize because of his general value to poetry. The result of all this was that
the Bollingen people awarded two prizes. Williams is said to be in
bad physical condition. I believed that he had had a stroke. But I
did not know that he had in fact had three strokes and is unable to
use his right side. Moreover, since he is now almost seventy, I imagined that when he retired he did so because he was able to live
modestly without being active. This appears to be untrue. He was
invited to act as consultant in poetry to the Library of Congress,
some time ago, and agreed to take on the job. I don't know how
much it pays but not a good deal. Then the rumors began to cir-
culate that he was a Communist and the people in Washington
have never allowed him to occupy his chair, so to speak. Of course,
I have no idea whether or not he is a Communist. But, since he is
a man who is interested in anything new that may be going
around, the chances are that he has interested himself in the subject
and I suppose that the only way to interest yourself in such a subject
is to associate with Communists. So far as Williams himself is
concerned, he is the least subversive man in the world. The question
in his case would not be what he would do but what his associates
would do. I am told that this experience is causing him a great deal
of anxiety. As I say, I have not the slightest knowledge of what the
facts are but I infer from the attitude of the people in Washington
that something has been discovered, which I regret because Williams is one of the few people in this country that really has an
active and constant interest in writing. Now, if something has been
discovered and his record is not clear, one wonders what effect this
may have on the Bollingen Prize which is already involved on
Pound's account. But I think that the Bollingen people and the government occupy different positions. I don't see how the government
can be expected to countenance any man who is committed to throw
bricks at it. Of all people, Williams would be the least justified in
throwing bricks at it anyhow because his case is typical of the philosophy with which America treats those who come to it from elsewhere. It is true that he was born in this country but neither one of
his parents were, unless I am mistaken.

Sincerely yours,
Wallace Stevens

Jan. 24 [1953]

My dear Wallachio:

I like your brief, promising letter. Promising a more prolonged communication and saltier commentaries. I have been reading a great deal: an attractive treatise on Esthetics: *Art as Expression* by J. Dewey; novels by Vittorini, refreshing and powerful as the Italian soil; Baudelaire's letters to his mother, Caroline Archimbaut-Dufays, really full of anguish, pain and desperation. ¡Remarkable relation, his with Mde. Aupick! Of France, I have *perused,* that is the exact term, Jean Tardieu, a good "modern" poet; Valery's latest book; Gide's *Journals,* quite a bore!;[1] but the wonderful, really delightful "discovery" was the reading of *Tom Jones.* In schools and colleges *Joseph Andrews* is the required reading. Why? Heavens knows! So I never got around [to] *Tom Jones.* It's really a great novel and one must be familiar with the picaresque novels of Spain—from the *Lazarillo de Tormes* down to Quevedo—to realize how well the English writers understood and brought about the literary transubstantiation. God, if any Catholic amigos were to hear me use that "sacred" term thus, there would be the hell to pay.

More news: T. S. Eliot's "Party" (how delightfully successful has become this minor piece!) has been done into Spanish.[2] It reads more archaic; quite silly, very silly indeed, to Catholic ears to read about his martyr and that silly (there I go again) mixture of psychoanalysis and metaphysics (?). Really, the master knows his theater and the piece, oh the little gem!, is really the right dish, should I say prescription for the empty American [?] a la reserche de something less material, or obvious. Truman Capote's *Other Voices, Other Rooms* has become *Otras Voces, Otros Ámbitos.*[3] I

1. Elio Vittorini's recent fiction: *Il Garofano Rosso* (Milan: Mondadori, 1948), *Le Donne di Messina* (Milan: Bompiani, 1949); *The Red Carnation* had just appeared in English (New York: New Directions, 1952). Baudelaire's *Lettres à sa mère* (Paris: Colmann-Lévy, 1944); possibly Jean Tardieu's *Le démon de l'irréalité* (Neuchâtel, 1946) or *Figures* (Paris: Gallimard, 1944); Valéry's (d. 1945) "latest book" in 1953, *Histoires Brisse* (Paris: Gallimard, 1950); Gide's *Journals, 1939–1942* and *1942–1949* (Paris: Gallimard, 1946 and 1950).

2. *The Cocktail Party* appeared in a Spanish translation by Jaime Tillo in *Revista de America* 23, no. 72 (1951).

3. Translated by Floreal Mazia (Buenos Aires: Editorial Sudamericana, 1950).

finally read the book and I found it quite good. The "man" has talent; let's hope he continues to write of that magical period, childhood. There were moods, sustained quite successfully, which evoked in my mind certain felicities of M. Alain-Fournier in *Le Grand Meaulnes*.[4] Of course, in his fiction there is the usual perversity inherent in an Episcopal or Baptist imagination—affinities to A. Gide in the episode of little Boris in *Les Faux-Monnayeurs*. By the way, I hear *Les Caves du Vatican* will be seen in New York City.[5] Dear God, how far will this *fiesta* last?

A friend of mine, recently arrived from Paris, the English painter, Osborne, brought news of that excellent Italian review you mentioned. I can't wait to see it!

Mariano will exhibit in the Feigl Gallery next month. I am told he will send you the invitation soon.

Please write soon. I feel quite lonely these days, with mother gone and any possibility of leaving Cuba more and more remote.

Yours with affection,
José

[Havana]
Sept. 10, 1954

Dear Wallachio:

I haven't written but often I think of you and of our encounters. Life has become difficult; so many things and persons I have esteemed have sort of left the front porch.

I begin to wonder: couldn't it be that I was always on the wrong track? To rectify now seems a bit silly. I hope however to have Cuba for a long time after. I get through a mess of business details which would leave Mother and myself in a quiet peacefull state of mind. Not much writing; lots of reading. To recommend: Count Keyserling's marvelous autobiography: Reise durch die Zeit 2 vols. He was a remarkable man and his friendships were numerous, interesting and very polemical.[1]

4. Paris: Emile-Paul, 1922.
5. *Les Faux Monnayeurs* (Paris: Gallimard, 1951). *Les Caves du Vatican* appeared in English translations as *The Vatican Swindlers* and *The Vatican Cellars* and was performed in New York.
1. A page is missing from this letter.

[Hartford, Connecticut]
December 15, 1954

Dear José:

It made me happy to receive your Christmas card and to hear about yourself and *Ciclón*. However, you failed to give me an address so that I have had to use the old one, which may or may not delay delivery to you.

About a week ago you were very much in my mind because, while I knew that you had left *Orígenes,* I did not know why and someone was asking me why. The real reason may be that you had outgrown the rather academic atmosphere of *Orígenes* and wanted to get under way with *Ciclón.* For my own part, I liked *Orígenes* and always made an effort to get something out of it although my Spanish is not much better than your Chinese. Do send me at least Number 1 of *Ciclón* and then, if it looks like anything that ought to interest an old man, I shall send you a subscription.

What a wonderful thing it is that you have been able to see the world to an extent that your trips to Europe and South America indicate. I suppose that between your perfect knowledge of English and Spanish you are able to assimilate the entire West as far as language goes. I wish I could say the same because, for a time at least, the West is now taking the lead. I can't say that that is true of music or that that is true of painting. But it seems to be true of literature. When I hear a piece of music and want to identify it, my first attempt is to do so by trying to fix the nationality of the musician. American music is slow, thin and often a bit affected as if music found its source in something other than the ordinary human being. And in painting I cannot see anything except imitation. Most American paintings are nothing but unpleasant color which does not seem to me to be in the least American. We need a few American masters in both music and painting before we can have any real identity.

This is intended to be nothing more than an attempt to communicate with you at Christmastime and to send you Christmas greetings and best wishes for the New Year. Sooner or later you will be coming to New York. When you do, let me know. I shall be glad to come down to spend a few hours with you.

Sincerely yours,
Wallace Stevens

La Habana, Cuba
Christmas Day, 1954

My dear Wallace:

I was delighted to receive your letter; a bit late because I had moved to Vedado and my sister lives now at our old home. I have the impression you don't like the idea of *Ciclón*. But wait and you will see. Of course, I do not want you to subscribe because to an old friend I would never think of asking to subscribe. It is true that *Orígenes* was becoming academic and anemic. I think *Ciclón* will cure this situation.

It was strange: I received your letter right after I was perusing the copy a friend of mine brought me from New York of your Collected Poems. I found the volume very handsome and so was your likeness in the frontispiece. Saludos y felicitaciones!

What you write of American music and painting is partly true. I think Mexican painting has given us that happy legitimate note which you miss in American painting. Tamayo, for instance, and the Cuban Lam are as good as anything you can find in Europe. And the music of Villalobos is neither thin nor academic. In the last issue of *New Mexico Quarterly* you will find a story of Jorge Luis Borges whom I esteem as original and fine as anything produced in Europe as far as fiction is concerned.[1] When Borges' *Ficciones* appeared in French, the critics raved: something very unusual in French critics when the matter concerns a foreign writer and South American more so. But remember that South America gave France a Lautremont and a Jules Superveille. And inspired the best writings of W. H. Hudson of *Green Mansions* and *The Purple Land*.[2] The tropics gave Monsieurs [Henri] Masson and [André] Breton some inspiring themes and to [Ronald] Firbank not a few succulent ideas for his satiric novels. So you see, my dear Wallace, that all is not so grey below the border.

Mother wants to take this opportunity to wish a Merry Christmas and to let you know that Pompilio, the loved burro, which she sold a few years ago, is still kicking about. She never forgets your card alluding to him. I hope your family is well. And that the rivers of

1. "Death and the Compass," *New Mexico Quarterly* 24, no. 3 (November 1954): 251–63.
2. London: Duckworth, 1904, and New York: Three Sirens Press, 1904.

Connecticut are not all frozen. Here the climate is lovely and your "paisanos" are starting to climb all over foamy Daiquiries.

Un abrazo,
Pepe

I am in an Insurance company (appropriate enough) but my present address is: Calle 23 no. 1516, Vedado, La Habana.

[Hartford, Connecticut]
February 15, 1955

Dear José:

Ciclón is large, not in size, but in portent. It contains three things that I am most interested in: [Ernesto] Sabato's article on abstract art, Cassou's on [Jorge] Guillén and [Julian] Marias' on the intellectual image of the world. I can only regret my inability to form more than a superficial impression of these. And I burn to read those fighting yellow pages inserted midway.

On the other hand, I am not crazy about the make-up nor the typography. Personally, I may attach more importance to these features than I should. But the appearance of a good thing makes it all the better.

Guillén will be better known before long than he is now. However, he needs much more competent expounding than he has had and the translations of his work have not been impressive. His fat Cantico[1] is one of the latest ornaments of my shelves.

Sincerely yours,
Wallace Stevens

1. Buenos Aires: Editorial Sudamericana, 1950.

INDEX

Beverly Coyle is Associate Professor of English at Vassar College and the author of *A Thought to be Rehearsed: Aphorism in Wallace Stevens's Poetry*. Alan Filreis is Assistant Professor of English at the University of Pennsylvania.

Library of Congress Cataloging-in-Publication Data
Stevens, Wallace, 1879–1955.
Secretaries of the moon.
Includes bibliographical references and index.
1. Stevens, Wallace, 1879–1955—Correspondence.
2. Poets, American—20th century—Correspondence.
3. Rodríguez Feo, José—Correspondence. 4. Editors—
Cuba—Correspondence. I. Rodríguez Feo, José.
II. Coyle, Beverly. III. Filreis, Alan, 1956–
IV. Title.
PS3537.T4753Z496   1986   811'.52 [B]   86-16835
ISBN 0-8223-0670-0